Yesterday,

December 7, 1941

—a date that will

live in infamy—

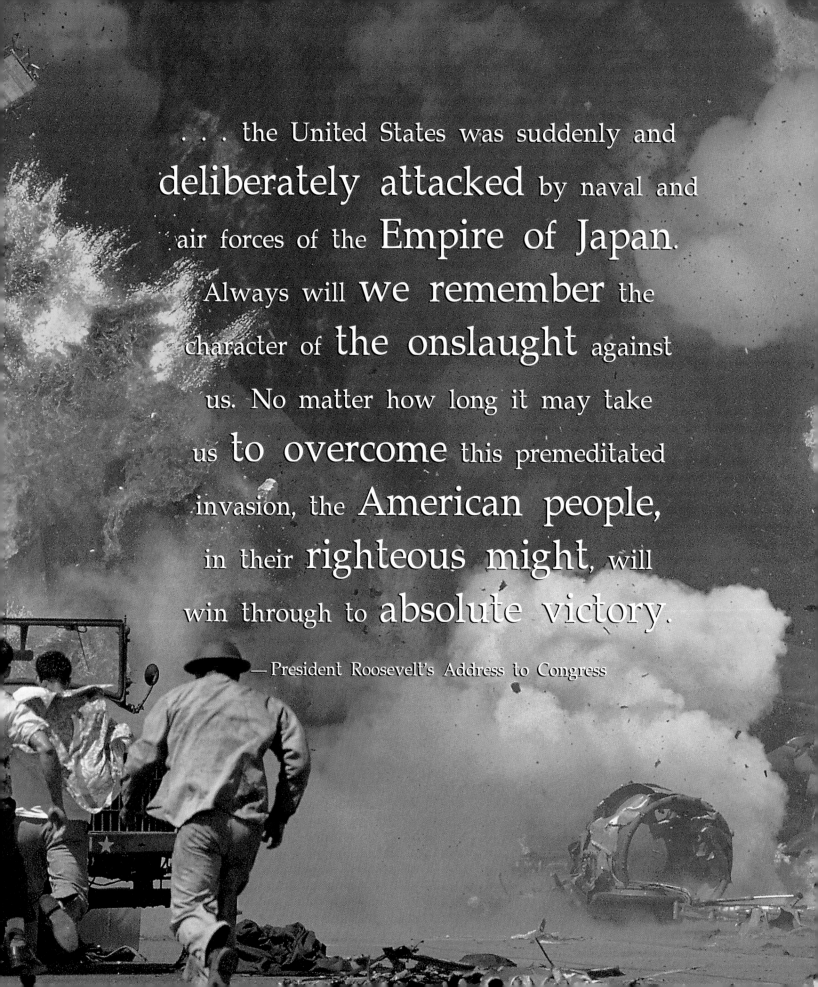

. . . the United States was suddenly and **deliberately attacked** by naval and air forces of the Empire of Japan. Always will we remember the character of the onslaught against us. No matter how long it may take us to overcome this premeditated invasion, the American people, in their righteous might, will win through to absolute victory.

—President Roosevelt's Address to Congress

PEARL HARBOR

THE MOVIE AND THE MOMENT

PHOTO FOREWORD BY
JERRY BRUCKHEIMER

INTRODUCTION BY
MICHAEL BAY

PREFACE BY
RANDALL WALLACE

EDITED BY
LINDA SUNSHINE AND **ANTONIA FELIX**

DESIGNED BY
TIMOTHY SHANER

BOXTREE

First published 2001 by Hyperion, New York

This edition published 2001 by Boxtree,
an imprint of Macmillan Publishers Ltd.,
25 Eccleston Place London SW1W 9NF
Basingstoke and Oxford
Associated companies throughout the world
www.macmillan.com

ISBN 0 7522 2002 0

A Newmarket Pictorial Moviebook: Produced by Newmarket Productions,
a division of Newmarket Publishing and Communications Company:
Esther Margolis, director; Frank DeMaio, production manager;
Keith Hollaman, editor. Edited by Linda Sunshine and Antonia Felix.
Designed by Timothy Shaner, Night & Day Design.

9 8 7 6 5 4 3 2 1

CREDITS

All photographs by Andrew Cooper, except as indicated below and in captions:
Jerry Bruckheimer: pages 8, 9, 10, 11, 82-83, 86-87, 98-101, 111, 112-113, 141,
146-147, 150; Larry Sultan: 12; Greg Gorman: 21; Chip Matheson: 142; Jack
Kney: 167; Richard Burton: 167; Pete Romano: 172-173. Digitally enhanced
images from Industrial Light and Magic: 74-75, 92-93, 168, 169, 170, 171.

Drawings: Simon Murton: pages 35, 36, 109; Aric Lasher: 36, 62, 63; Susan Burig: 37;
Nigel Phelps: 44- 45; Rick Buoen: 48, 57, 109; Eric Rosenberg: 63; Warren Manser:
106-107, 142, 154; Robert Consing (storyboards): 124-125; Bill Skinner: 127; Guy
Hendrix Dyas: 108, 136-137, 144, 174-175; Michael Kaplan: 143, 161, 162-163.

Permission to reprint copyrighted material from the following sources is gratefully
acknowledged. The publisher has made every effort to contact copyrights holders;
any errors or omissions are inadvertent and will be corrected upon notice in
future reprintings.

Page 1: © Liysa King/Pacific Stock. 47, 52 (Yamamoto portrait), 83: U.S. Naval
Historical Center. 49: Maps.Com (map). 56: Map by Albert D. McJoynt from
The Way It Was: Pearl Harbor by Donald M. Goldstein, Katherine V. Dillon
and J. Michael Wenger © 1991 Brassey's, Inc. 86: Survivor account posted on
execpc.com/~dschaaf (Pearl Harbor: Remembered), reprinted with permission of
Don Schaaf and Betty Mortensen. 90: Franklin D. Roosevelt Library. 97: Excerpt
from *In and Out of Harm's Way* by Capt. Doris M. Sterner, reprinted with author's
permission. 108: Courtesy of the *Seattle Post-Intelligencer* Collection, Museum of
History and Industry. 114 & 115: *New York Times* front page and excerpts reprinted
with permission of the *New York Times*. 115: *Honolulu Star-Bulletin* (front page
reprint); Thomas McAvoy/TimePix (Roosevelt photograph). 44, 45, 46, 58,
59, 63, 66, 79, 80, 86, 87, 105, 107, 115, 118, 123: National Archives and
Records Administration.

A CIP catalogue record for this book is available from the British Library.

Printed and bound in the United States.

CONTENTS

PHOTO FOREWORD

BY JERRY BRUCKHEIMER

LEFT and BOTTOM RIGHT: Photographs by Jerry Bruckheimer. TOP RIGHT: Portrait by Andrew Cooper.

More than anybody, Jerry understood what was owed to the people who actually experienced this Pearl Harbor. I think he really cared that this be done in the right way and not be a fast-food movie. He wanted it to be resonant and significant and be remembered in the Pantheon of good movies that tell a story of the Second World War.

—BEN AFFLECK

LEFT and ABOVE: Photographs by Jerry Bruckheimer.

INTRODUCTION

BY MICHAEL BAY

It happened on a Sunday morning. The attack on Pearl Harbor lasted just two hours, but those have proven to be among the most pivotal hours in American history.

Pearl Harbor woke us up as a nation; it showed that America was no longer a fortress of peace and innocence. A generation was called upon to wage a massive world war on two different sides of the globe.

In early conceptual stages of the movie, I met with many survivors who were surprised by the falling bombs in peaceful Hawaii. As I listened to their stories and stared into their tears, I knew this was a movie that had to be told for America and the world. This was a very special generation, which was willing to place their country above themselves.

Choosing to make *Pearl Harbor* was a huge, life-changing decision as a director. There was a battle within me—I wondered if this epic attack could ever be re-created. Maybe there was a good reason why no one has attempted to make this movie in the thirty years since *Tora Tora Tora*.

Quick research showed me that there is only one original flying Japanese Zero in the world and very few ships from that era. How could anyone be crazy enough to tackle this movie? Maybe I should just do that safe, small, character film, I thought. But I kept thinking of those tears on those old cheeks. The powerful images I got from the survivors kept swirling in my head. During a trip to Pearl Harbor, walking around Ford Island, where the brunt of the attack happened, and totally immersed in my director mode, I had a quiet moment to myself where I realized that under my shoes were the Japanese strafing bullet holes in the cement. This was hallowed ground and I was lucky to even be here; it was a moment I had to seize—to power through the wars to get this movie to the screen.

As I got deeper and deeper into my research, I learned that historians have different

LEFT: Photo of Michael Bay on location by Larry Sultan.

I love directing. This is one of those movies that it is worth two years of my life. I always dreamed of being a film director and this is an amazing story that I am honored to tell.

—MICHAEL BAY

Working with Michael is a challenge. He makes you want to run in his wake. I don't think anyone could catch up with his energy but every day we gave it our best shot.

—ALEC BALDWIN

I think what is really going to surprise people is the level to which Michael went to make a classic, epic romance. Even I was surprised by some of the cut footage that I saw and I was there, I was in the scene.

—BEN AFFLECK

Michael Bay brings spontaneity to everything. You might think you know what he's going to want but when you get to work in the morning, he'll have a whole different twist on it. It's always exciting. Michael is going to push everyone on the crew to their utmost. There are no light days on a Michael Bay film.

—K. C. HODENFIELD, ASSOCIATE PRODUCER/FIRST ASSISTANT DIRECTOR

views and theories about what happened at Pearl. The Pentagon, which worked closely with me on this movie, admitted that there were no real Navy or Army logs kept during this time period. And even the men and women who were actually in the attack have varying accounts of what happened. Everyone seemed to be an expert, but every story was different. The question became: Would I be able to satisfy every survivor, historian, and military buff? The answer was no.

My job as a director was to take the various stories and themes and, working very closely with the writer, Randall Wallace, give the audience the overall essence of the attack on Pearl Harbor. Randall created characters based on pieces of real people we met; these are characters that we can fall in love with, and see through their eyes what it must have been like during this harrowing time.

I took two years out of my life to make this movie. But I knew from the beginning, when I first stared into the survivors' tears, that my efforts and the efforts of my amazing crew would pay off. I have a vivid memory of showing the crew around Ford Island during preproduction. We came upon a plaque directly across from the sunken *Arizona*, marking the spot where a torpedo hit nearly six decades ago. My crew stood in silence for three minutes at the sight of this small monument. It was a solemn moment for all of us, and I think it helped the crew appreciate the undertaking were about to begin.

I recently showed the film's trailer to

Michael is very clever at making stunts look bigger than they are by bringing elements close to the camera and by using selective focus. He is the master at creating more mayhem than there really is. If he has to, Michael can make a traffic jam with just one car.

—JOHN SCHWARTZMAN, A.S.C. DIRECTOR OF PHOTOGRAPHY

seventy-five survivors; when the lights came on, I saw that again many had tears in their eyes. One of them leaned over to me and whispered, "I'm so proud that someone did this film. My one wish is to be able to go back, but I don't think I'll be around that long because my heart isn't so good." I hope that man makes it, because this movie is dedicated to him, and to everyone who was at Pearl Harbor on that fateful Sunday morning.

Pearl Harbor is not just a place in Hawaii; it is an unforgettable landmark in history. There's a timeless lesson in our story, a testament to the human spirit; that even after terrible calamity, people can pull together and rise up from the ashes. When all the survivors are gone, this film will be a tribute to their memories, and to the values they stood for. Too often nowadays, we forget what it is like to believe in something greater than ourselves.

PREFACE

BY RANDALL WALLACE

The original working title of this film was *Tennessee*, and in that little fact is the story of my involvement with *Pearl Harbor*.

I first met Michael Bay at a dinner given by the Directors Guild of America. He was still hot off the success of *Armageddon*, and I was busy planning my next project after *Man in the Iron Mask*, my first film as a director. Michael was familiar with my writing on *Braveheart*, and we had a good time chatting for a few minutes. We agreed that it might be fun to work together sometime, but I didn't imagine how soon that would be.

A few days later my agent, Dave Wirtschafter, called me to say that the folks at Disney wanted to make a movie about Pearl Harbor, and they wondered if I'd like to work with Michael and Jerry Bruckheimer on the project.

I met Jerry and was impressed by his energy and determination, not to mention his amazing track record with producing commercial films. He and Michael had enjoyed great success at making modern movies together; my reputation was built on historical epics; we all figured that a collaboration might result in something exciting. The folks at Disney thought so too.

But before we plunged into such a big undertaking, I wanted to assure myself and everyone else that our differing sensibilities would mix. So I offered them a deal: I'd go home and work on a story, looking for characters and a tale that I could be passionate about. I'd come back and tell them what I'd hit on, and if they didn't like what I'd come up with, they didn't owe me a thing; if they did like it, we were in business. This sounded good to everybody—so off I went.

As I mulled over Pearl Harbor, what most interested me was the power of patriotism, how it had driven our country and others into global war. One of the many unique aspects of the events of December 7, 1941, was the fact that they transformed America from a nation that wanted to isolate itself from war into a nation that would not cease fighting until it was victorious. This enormous change occurred in a single morning, inside the hearts of Americans.

I asked myself how to frame such a story; where does a telling of a tale about Pearl Harbor begin, and where does it end? And for that I had to think about the characters. Who were the people who went to war? Why did they try to ignore Germany's aggression in Europe, and Japan's in Asia? Why did Pearl Harbor make such a difference to Americans? And what events best demonstrate their response?

The truth is, the process wasn't that analytical. Writing comes from the passions and prejudices, like love does. My parents had lived through this time; their love for each other was born then, back in Tennessee, where some years after World War II I was born. I began to dream about people much like them, and from those dreams came Rafe, Danny, and Evelyn.

I went back and told Michael, Jerry, and the folks at Disney about these new characters, and the way I imagined them falling in love. I told them about my childhood home in Tennessee, the Volunteer State, where there is a tradition among people that tells them to step forward freely, to choose the hard road, to volunteer. Todd Garner,

the Disney executive who first came up with the original idea of doing the film, said, "Until we title this movie publicly, let's call it *Tennessee*."

I wasn't involved with the actual filming; I spent that time writing a novel based on my original screenplay. I love the world that leaps to life within the imagination of a good reader. But I love movies too, and I, like so many others around the world, am waiting with great anticipation to see Evelyn, Danny, and Rafe walk across the screen, and live and love through the terrifying darkness and brilliant light that surrounded Pearl Harbor.

RAFE

BEN AFFLECK

DANNY

EVELYN

KATE BECKINSALE

JOSH HARTNETT

THE CAST

GENERAL DOOLITTLE

ALEC BALDWIN

DORIE MILLER

CUBA GOODING, JR.

FDR

JON VOIGHT

AMERICAN INNOCENCE

AMERICA: 1941

Before the Pearl Harbor attack, America had seen more than two decades of peace. The Great War that ended in 1918 had redrawn the map of Europe, cost more than 116,000 lives and left more than 200,000 wounded. Memories of the war were largely responsible for the nation's isolationist attitude. Even though Americans abhorred the rise of dictatorships in Europe and sympathized with China's plight against the Japanese, a majority was opposed to becoming involved in an overseas conflict again. In addition, grave issues facing Americans at home in the 1930s forced millions to struggle with day-to-day survival, leaving little time to contemplate foreign politics. America was primarily a small-town nation at the time, with most people living in towns of fewer than 25,000. To many citizens, European and Asian conflicts appeared too remote to consider.

Millions of Americans lost their jobs during the Depression, and in 1940 nearly ten million were still out of work. The vicious cycle of decline rolled on: businesses faltered, sales fell, production decreased and employees were let go—causing sales to fall even more and beginning the process again. Even nature turned against the country in the 1930s, delivering a

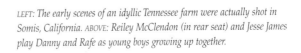

LEFT: *The early scenes of an idyllic Tennessee farm were actually shot in Somis, California.* ABOVE: *Reiley McClendon (in rear seat) and Jesse James play Danny and Rafe as young boys growing up together.*

HAWAII: LIFE ON THE BASE

In 1941, the Territory of Hawaii was one of America's favorite vacation spots. Tourism made up one-third of the islands' economy and rooms in the best waterfront hotels cost $22 a night.

An American presence was well established. About one-fourth of the population were white residents, members of long established wealthy families. The other 60 percent were Asian, primarily Japanese and Chinese. A mere 15 percent of the 415,000 island people were native Hawaiians.

Much of Oahu's appearance reflected the simple architectural style of the New England missionaries who settled there in the early 1900s, with white churches and a notable absence of billboards. Island life was casual and focused on the outdoors. Stores and shops closed at four in the afternoon and Honolulu shut down at midnight, even on weekends.

Strategically, Hawaii was the United States' most forward possession in the Pacific. The U.S. Pacific fleet had been based in Pearl Harbor since 1940, and guns and cannons buried in mountains had earned Hawaii the nickname "Gibraltar of the Pacific."

When you're doing an historical picture, it's very rare that you get to shoot in the actual place where it happened. Setting up shots, you suddenly realize, oh yeah, sixty years ago a Zero came right down through that canyon—it gives you goose bumps. One night at the hotel, our valet— he was old enough to be around in 1941—told us that when he heard our bombs in the harbor and saw the Zeros overhead, he dragged his wife outside and said to her, "They're back."

—JOHN FRAZIER,
SPECIAL EFFECTS SUPERVISOR

ABOVE: *Ewen Brenner as Red.*
LEFT: *Re-creating life in Hawaii before the attack.*

33

Nearly 43,000 soldiers were posted on the Hawaiian Islands in 1941, and most of these were on various bases on Oahu. Airfields and military buildings were ringed by countryside. Whenever they could, servicemen headed for Honolulu to drink at the Black Cat Café or the Two Jacks, watch a variety show at the Princess or amble down Hotel Street with its dance halls, shooting galleries, tattoo parlors and pinball machines. In December 1941, the Army and Navy were on alert, but this status

had become so ordinary that for many soldiers, evenings and time off followed the usual routine.

The bases provided entertainment for servicemen, too. The most popular spot at Pearl Harbor was the Navy's Bloch Recreation Center, where soldiers could play pool, watch boxing matches, dance, listen to live music and drink 3.2 beer. A favorite event was the battle of the bands, and the Saturday night before the Japanese attack, bands from four ships battled it out for the Fleet Band Championships.

The band from the USS *Pennsylvania* won, but they would never get to their final match against the USS *Arizona*. A few hours later, every member of the *Arizona* band would be killed when a Japanese bomb blasted their ship.

FAR LEFT: *Beach scene from the movie showing life in Hawaii.* ABOVE: *Concept drawing of the barracks on Ford Island by Simon Murton.* ABOVE RIGHT: *Tom Sizemore as Earl.* BELOW: *Squadron barracks showing the explosion in the gym on the bottom left. Drawing by Simon Murton.*

The Hula-La Bar was interesting because we needed a
live set for one of the lighter moments in the movie. As
it was a Hawaiian surfer bar, we had a good excuse
to build something frivolous. We had this set that
incorporated a large hula girl and her skirt becomes
the main part of the bar where everyone sits.

—NIGEL PHELPS, PRODUCTION DESIGNER

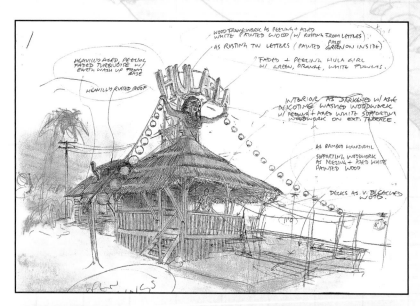

FAR LEFT: Simon Murton's early concept illustrations of the Hula-La Bar and a photo of the finished set as it appears in the movie. CENTER: Blueprints of the 30-foot-tall Hula-La Bar by Aric Lasher. TOP ABOVE: Ben Affleck and his co-stars in a scene shot inside the bar. ABOVE: Location photo of the Los Angeles beach cove where the Hula-La Bar was constructed. As the set was built on sand very close to the ocean, the production team was apprehensive that the high tide would damage it. BOTTOM RIGHT: Graphic designer Susan Burig created cocktail napkins for the tables. Table lamps of hula dancers with swiveling hips were rented as props for the tables (shown in the movie still).

EAGLE SQUADRON

From May through October 1940, Americans listened to radio reports of the Battle of Britain that raged in the skies overseas. Accounts of Royal Air Force pilots, in their Spitfires and Hurricanes, battling the Germans made many young American men anxious to cross the ocean and join in the fight. Due to the heavy loss of RAF pilots, by the summer of 1940 the call went out for volunteers. Thousands of Yanks applied, but only a fraction—244—were accepted into the RAF Fighter Command Numbers 71, 121 and 133: The Eagle Squadrons.

An organization called the Knight Committee recruited pilots for these volunteer units. Requirements were somewhat less strict than those for the U.S. Army Air Corps, which made the prospect of joining up even more attractive. Potential recruits had to be between the ages of 20 and 31, have 20/40 eyesight that was correctable to 20/20, a college education or a high school diploma; no flying experience was required. Most recruits did not have military experience or a college education. They wanted to get into the action and experience

LEFT: Josh Hartnett (right) escorts Ben Affleck to the train that will begin his journey to England to join an Eagle Squadron. The scene was shot in Union Station in Los Angeles.

aerial combat. American pilot Robert Patterson wrote, "I joined the RAF not primarily for patriotic reasons. We all knew a war was coming. I used this as a quick way for some flying excitement." High adventure, combat flying, the romantic notion of being a wartime flying ace and a desire to help the British all played a part in motivating America's pilots to volunteer.

Once accepted, the new recruits went to England to undergo flight training in RAF planes at an operational training unit (OTU). These training programs ran from two to four weeks. Most went through the entire RAF flight-training program, putting in 200 hours of flying time.

In addition to becoming skilled in the cockpits of Spitfires and Hurricanes, American pilots had to learn the standard formations and tactics being used by the RAF. Formations included line astern, in which three lines of four planes were spaced 200 to 300 yards apart. Each line of four planes was named white, red or blue flight. RAF tactics that the Americans had envisioned while listening to radio reports now became part of their own piloting skills: get in close, fire in short bursts, use height for advantage, turn to face an attack, maintain high cover, hit hard quickly and get out.

The RAF made it policy that the squadron and flight commanders in the Eagle Squadrons would be Englishmen, and 16 British pilots served in these positions. From the formation of the first Eagle Squadron in September 1940 until the squadrons were incorporated into the U.S. Army Air Corps two years later, the Eagle Squadrons:
• destroyed 73 German planes
• lost 77 American and 5 British pilots

The day after the attack on Pearl Harbor, the Eagle Squadrons sent representatives to the American Embassy in London to offer their services in the U.S. Air Corps. It would take several months before the American headquarters was set up in London, however, and the pilots remained in the Eagle Squadrons fighting in the European arena of the war.

America's entrance into World War II called for the Eagle Squadrons to become part of the newly formed U.S. Army Air Corps command in Britain. Many issues had to be ironed out to make this possible, such as the rankings the Eagle Squadron pilots would receive once they became part of the American military. None of the pilots had served in the Army Air Corps; therefore they didn't have U.S. pilot's wings. General Spaatz, commander of the American Air Corps headquarters in London, ordered that they be given their wings upon transfer to the American forces and, in most cases, given rank equivalent to what they held in the RAF. The general hoped to spread the experienced Eagle Squadron pilots among his various new units, but the Eagles insisted upon staying together.

On September 29, 1942, the Eagle Squadrons were transferred into the Fourth Fighter Group of the U.S. Army Air Corps, becoming the 334th (formerly 71st), 335th (121st) and 336th (133rd).

BELOW AND FAR RIGHT: RAF scenes were shot at the Badminton estate located outside of Bath, England. Photos by Frank Connor.

THE EAGLE SQUADRON WORLD

SLANG

BIG NOISE . . . . Important person
BUS DRIVER . . . . Bomber pilot
CRAB ALONG, TO . . . . To fly near the ground or water
DEAD BEAT . . . . RAF non-flying personnel
FIREWORKS, MR. . . . . Armaments Officer
GLAMOUR BOYS . . . . Fighter pilots
GRAVY . . . . Gasoline
HEDGE-HOP, TO . . . . To fly so low the aircraft appears
to be hopping over hedges
HOOCH, TO . . . . To pub-crawl, drink at bars
MAE WEST . . . . Life-saving stole or waistcoat,
inflated if wearer falls into the sea
OFFICE . . . . Cockpit of aircraft
PULPIT . . . . Cockpit of aircraft
QUICK SQUIRT . . . . Short, sharp burst of fire
SPROG . . . . Brand new uniform; newly commissioned officer
TAIL-END CHARLEY . . . . Rear gunner in a large bombing aircraft,
or the pilot of rear aircraft in formation
TAPES . . . . Non-commissioned officers' stripes
TIDDLY . . . . Intoxicated
TOUCH BOTTOM, TO . . . . To crash

Badge showing the Eagle Squadron "Boxing Eagle." It was drawn by artists at the Walt Disney Studios, who designed many such insignias during the course of the war.

MISSIONS

RHUBARB   A two-plane mission in which pilots made low-level ground attacks. Flying just a few feet off the ground, they shot up tanks, shops, railroads, troops or any other military targets.

BALBOA   In this mission, fighter planes served as decoys while bombers hit a nearby target. Many Balboa missions were flown over German-occupied targets in Belgium and France.

CONVOY ESCORT PATROL   Usually two planes flying circuits around ships at low altitude—sometimes as low as 100 feet. Convoy escorts were long and monotonous, and fog and poor weather accounted for many escort planes crashing into the sea.

CIRCUS   Designed to draw out the Luftwaffe, this was a combined bomber and fighter mission.

RAMROD   An escort mission for bombers such as B-17s and Blenheims.

RODEO   A fighter sweep, usually flown by a three-squadron wing when the mission flew from a large base. Squadrons based at smaller fields flew solo sweeps.

THE NURSES OF PEARL HARBOR

The day of the Japanese attack, 119 Army and Navy nurses were stationed at Pearl Harbor. Only registered nurses qualified for military service at the time, and because of their professional training every nurse had officer status (but received less pay than male officers). Duty on the Hawaiian Islands was hard work during the months that preceded the attack, with emergency drills and other activities that went along with being on alert, but everyone agreed it was a heav-

enly post. Nurses were treated to formal dances at the officers' clubs and open house parties at the homes of wealthy Hawaiian residents. They enjoyed golfing, tennis, sight-seeing, and dating—in an island paradise where the ratio of men to women was about 10,000 to 1.

The surprise attack that early Sunday morning shook the entire medical community into action, although for many it took a few minutes to realize what was happening.

As described in *G.I. Nightingales* by Barbara Tomblin,

Army Nurse Myrtle Watson was wheeling patients out to the second-story porch of the hospital at Schofield Barracks that morning. At about 7:45, she and a wounded soldier named Jack stood on the porch looking over the field, when the air suddenly became filled with

ABOVE: A scene from the beginning of the movie shows the nurses arriving for the first time on Pearl Harbor. The five featured actresses are (from left) Catherine Kellner, James King, Kate Beckinsale, Sarah Rue and Jennifer Garner. RIGHT: Kate Beckinsale on location in Hawaii.

roaring planes. Jack, a sergeant, recognized the planes as Japanese and said to Nurse Watson, "Chick, I think we're at war!"

"I said in a rather shaky voice," the nurse recalled, "'We couldn't be at war; someone would tell us.' We just stood frozen in our places, staring at the sky as the planes made their runs. The effect was almost hypnotic."

Stationed at Hickam Field, Army Nurse Monica Counter began treating her first patients about ten minutes after the first attack. "The sight in our hospital I'll never forget," she wrote in a letter published in *We're In This War, Too*. "No arms, no legs, intestines hanging out, etc."

While she worked, every sound was drowned out by the deafening noise of bombs, machine guns, and antiaircraft fire. The barracks surrounding the hospital were engulfed in flames.

In the harbor, nestled near the *Arizona* and the *Nevada*, the USS *Solace* hospital ship was flooded with wounded during the attack. Nurses and doctors went into high gear, aware every moment that *Solace* could meet the same fate as the burning and sinking ships beside them. "We could hear the fighting raging," recalled the chief nurse, Grace Lally. "But our job was inside the ship, and there we stayed for ten days."

CALMNESS AND COURAGE

The first Army nurse to be awarded the Purple Heart was 1st Lt. Annie G. Fox, the chief nurse on duty at Hickam Field during the Pearl Harbor attack. The citation recognized "her fine example of calmness, courage, and leadership, which was of great benefit to the morale of all she came in contact with."

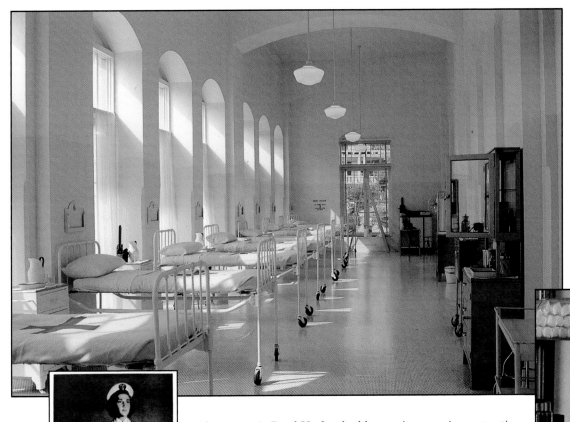

FAR LEFT: *The nurses in uniform: Catherine Kellner, Sarah Rue, James King, Jennifer Garner and Kate Beckinsale.* NEAR LEFT: *The interior of the hospital that was filmed in Los Angeles, California.* BOTTOM LEFT: *Concept drawing of the hospital ward by Nigel Phelps.* BELOW: *Kate Beckinsale.*

WANTED MORE NAVY NURSES
Be a commissioned officer in the U. S. Navy
For information write: The Surgeon General, Navy Dept., Washington, D.C.

The nurses in Pearl Harbor had harrowing experiences treating these burned and dying young men without enough medical supplies. The heroics of these women are no different from the men who tried desperately to defend that small island.

—JERRY BRUCKHEIMER

PEARL HARBOR HOSPITAL WARD

As for the hospital, we shot the grounds in Hawaii but we came back to L.A. to shoot the interiors and the entrance, all of which was going to get blown up. By doing this in L.A. we would have much more control over the explosions. We shot in Linda Vista, downtown, where we built this 120-foot-long ward and the entrance onto the existing location.

—NIGEL PHELPS, PRODUCTION DESIGNER

BATTLESHIP ROW

Hawaii was selected as the new home for the U.S. Pacific Fleet in May 1940 for several reasons. The United States needed to have battleships stationed in a mid-ocean port to protect the Philippines and to guard the canal in Panama. Pearl Harbor lies 3,430 nautical miles southeast of Tokyo, approximately 2,000 nautical miles west to southwest of San Francisco and 4,767 nautical miles east of Manila. The islands were surrounded by vast expanses of ocean that would, theoretically, allow adequate time to locate and engage any incoming naval forces. In addition to being impregnable, Hawaii was in good proximity to other bases being built up by the United States—Midway, Wake, Johnston Island and Palmyra.

From the pivot point of Hawaii, the fleet could set out in any direction at a moment's notice. Moving in and out of the harbor in stately maneuvers, the enormous fleet was a source of pride to the entire country. Nine battleships, three aircraft carriers, 21 cruisers, 53 destroyers, 23 submarines, dozens of minesweepers, target ships and auxiliary vessels filled the harbor and nearby waters.

No expense had been spared to make Pearl Harbor an independent maintenance base with dry docks, workshops, oil storage tanks and other installations, and confidence ran high with the state of the ground forces as well. The Army, with 43,000 troops engaged in continual field exercises and armed with the latest modern warfare equipment, claimed that Pearl Harbor was "the best defended naval base in the world." Fighter plane squadrons gleamed at Wheeler Field and bomber planes filled the hangars and air strips at Hickam Field. A virtual citadel, Oahu was dotted with field guns, antiaircraft guns and cannons.

ABOVE and FAR LEFT: Archival photographs taken in Japanese planes of Ford Island during the opening moments of the attack on Pearl Harbor. BELOW: Color studies by Robert Woodruff for the various ships stationed at Pearl Harbor on December 7, 1941.

Many of the structures at Pearl Harbor were new, having been built after 1939.

The only entrance to the harbor was through a channel that had been blasted through the coral reef. This channel was 375 yards wide and 3,500 yards long with a minimum depth of 45 feet. The military was acutely aware that if a large ship sank in the channel, it would block the harbor for an indefinite time and prevent any ships from entering or leaving Pearl Harbor.

The Department of the Army in Hawaii was divided into three principal segments: two infantry divisions and supporting troops making up the beach and land defense forces; the Coast Artillery command, consisting of the sea-

47

coast and fixed antiaircraft units along the coasts in permanent fortifications; and the Hawaiian Air Force, housed on Hickam, Wheeler, Haleiwa, and Bellows Fields.

Pearl Harbor's two top commanders, the Army's Lieutenant General Walter C. Short and Navy's Admiral Husband E. Kimmel, became friends at their new post and played golf together every other Sunday. As commanding general, Hawaiian Department, General Short led the forces responsible for protecting the fleet in Hawaii. Short's Army career, which began in 1902, had taken him through the battlefields of World War I, infantry regiments throughout the world, several years in Washington and a variety of command assignments. In Hawaii, General Short's duty also covered the overall air command, which included the Hawaiian Air Force.

Admiral Kimmel, commander in chief, U.S. Pacific Fleet, assumed command in Hawaii in February 1941. He was an early replacement for Admiral James O. Richardson, who was relieved from his post after strong disagreements with President Roosevelt over the fleet's move from San Diego to Hawaii. A diligent officer with a sterling career as a battleship commander and director of ship movements in Washington, Admiral Kimmel devoted his command to readying the fleet for offensive battle. By all accounts, he believed the Pacific Fleet would be engaged in offensive maneuvers and never be in a defensive position. Like military leaders in Washington, Kimmel believed that Hawaii was "impregnable."

TOP: Concept drawing by Rick Buoen of a peaceful Pearl Harbor before the attack. BELOW: Early drawings of the ships at Pearl with production notes about what happens to each vessel. RIGHT: Detailed list of every ship at Pearl on the morning of the attack, along with a map showing exactly where each ship was positioned.

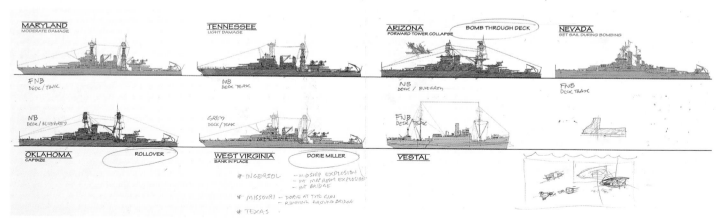

PEARL HARBOR 0755, DECEMBER 7, 1941

Ships in Pearl Harbor on Sunday morning,
December 7, 1940 (96 total)

Battleships
USS *Arizona*
USS *Pennsylvania*
USS *California*
USS *Tennessee*
USS *Maryland*
USS *West Virginia*
USS *Oklahoma*
USS *Nevada*
(9 based at Pearl Harbor; 8 there for the attack)

Cruisers
USS *New Orleans* (heavy cruiser)
USS *San Francisco* (heavy cruiser)
USS *St. Louis* (light cruiser)
USS *Helena* (light cruiser)
USS *Raleigh* (light cruiser)
USS *Detroit* (light cruiser)
USS *Honolulu* (light cruiser)
USS *Phoenix* (light cruiser)
(21 based at Pearl Harbor; 8 there for the attack)

Destroyers
USS *Allen*, USS *Aylwin*, USS *Bagley*, USS *Blue*, USS *Case*,
USS *Cassin*, USS *Chew*, USS *Conyngham*, USS *Cummings*,
USS *Dale*, USS *Dewey*, USS *Downes*, USS *Farragut*, USS
Helm, USS *Henley*, USS *Worden*, USS *Hull*, USS *Jarvis*, USS
MacDonough, USS *Monaghan*, USS *Montgomery*, USS *Breese*,
USS *Mugford*, USS *Patterson*, USS *Phelps*, USS *Ralph Talbot*,
USS *Ramsay*, USS *Reid*, USS *Schley*, USS *Selfridge*, USS *Shaw*,
USS *Sicard*, USS *Tracy*, USS *Tucker*, USS *Ward*
(53 based at Pearl Harbor; 35 there for the attack)

Submarines
USS *Narwhal*, USS *Dolphin*,
USS *Cachelot*, USS *Tautog*
(23 based at Pearl Harbor; 4 there for the attack)

Additional vessels in the harbor:
Minelayers, Seaplane-tenders, Repair ships, Target
ships (i.e., USS *Utah*)

All three aircraft carriers—USS *Lexington*, USS *Saratoga*
and USS *Enterprise*—were at sea.

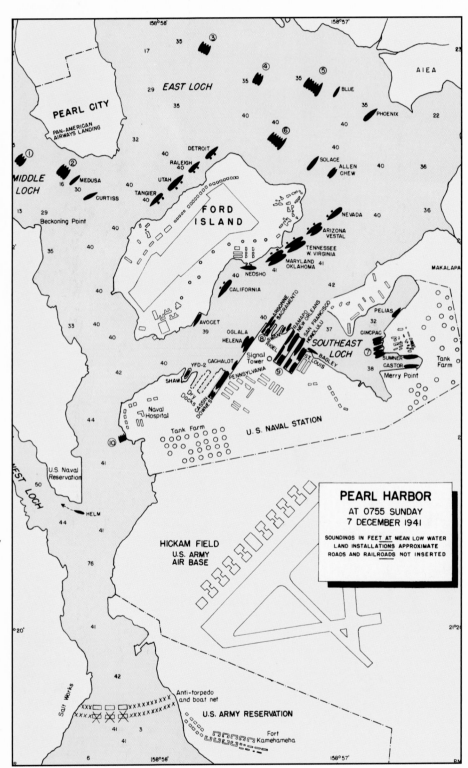

JAPAN
JOURNEY TO WAR

The road to war between Japan and the United States was paved throughout the tumultuous decade of the 1930s. Japan was one of the first nations to feel and react to the worldwide economic depression ignited by the American stock market crash of 1929. Poor in natural resources, Japan responded by seizing Manchuria and embarking upon a mission to lead the "Greater East Asia Co-Prosperity Sphere." With this policy, Japan hoped to exploit anti-Western sentiment throughout Asia, push out British, Dutch and French holders of Far East possessions and become the overall protectorate of Asia. China and other Asian nations saw the economic and imperialistic motivations behind Japan's policy, however, and did not openly embrace Japan's fer-

vent call that "Asia belongs to the Asians."

The Manchurian occupation began in the autumn of 1931, and Japanese troops soon launched a full-scale military attack on the Chinese in that region. After winning control of all of Manchuria the following year, the Japanese army declared it an independent state, renaming it Manchukuo. The League of Nations refused to acknowledge this puppet state, and Japan withdrew from the league in

LEFT: According to production designer Nigel Phelps, director Michael Bay often wanted the production design to tell a story in one image. This set was meant to establish the Japanese war counsel without relying on subtitles. The scene was filmed in a gun emplacement in San Pedro, California, which was built in the early 1940s as a coastal defense. The Japanese flag (original drawing below) instantly established the location.

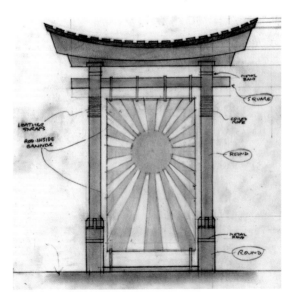

YAMAMOTO

In the first weeks of 1941, Admiral Isoroku Yamamoto told a fellow officer: "If we are to have war with America, we will have no hope of winning unless the U.S. fleet in Hawaiian waters can be destroyed." Although he had long been opposed to going to war with the United States and Britain, Yamamoto put his opinions aside when his country decided that war was the only option and crafted a strategy he believed was Japan's only chance of success. His plan, although unpopular with the rest of the Imperial Navy, was to make a large-scale, carrier-launched surprise attack that would cripple the Pacific fleet. Yamamoto eventually succeeded in selling the plan to his superiors and implemented a detailed preparation strategy that gave the strike force an excellent chance of success.

Like several other top naval officers, Yamamoto knew America well. He had attended Harvard for two years, from 1917 to 1919, and served as a naval attaché in the Japanese embassy in Washington from 1925 to 1928. These long stints in the United States convinced him that this nation would be a superior opponent, and a preemptive strike would be Japan's only possible chance of gaining the advantage in a war in the Pacific.

Yamamoto's career in the Royal Imperial Navy was a steady progression of promotions and important posts following his grad-uation from the naval academy at Etajima at age 20. Just one year after graduation, he received serious injuries—including losing two fingers on his left hand—while serving on a cruiser during the Battle of Tsushima in the Russo-Japanese War.

In his village, the young lieutenant commander was revered as a rising star of the military. Born Isoroku Takano, he was adopted after both his parents died, according to Japanese custom. At age 30 he became a member of the wealthy, prominent Yamamoto clan, and married soon after.

At Harvard, Yamamoto polished his English, developed an in-depth knowledge of the American oil industry, became an avid poker player and read everything he could find about the newest war weapon—the airplane. After touring airplane factories and studying air action reports of the European war, he was convinced that the future of war was in air power. This conviction would bring Yamamoto into bitter conflict with the Japanese military establishment, which had invested itself heavily in battleship-style warfare.

Upon his return from Harvard, Yamamoto got his first big command as captain of the fledgling Japanese naval air training school. There he learned to fly and began implementing training programs and policies that would earn him recognition as Japan's father of avi-

I'm not sure Yamamoto believed in what he was doing but his country ordered him to supervise the attack and he was a man on a mission. We had a oil embargo against Japan at the time. With only about eighteen months' worth of oil left, they figured that attacking us was one way to end the embargo. We decided to present the Japanese as the brilliant strategists that they were. Their attack caught us completely off guard and accomplished everything they planned. Luckily for us, they failed to wipe us out completely only because three of our carriers were at sea.

—JERRY BRUCKHEIMER

ation. When he was promoted to rear admiral, Yamamoto dramatically stepped up aviation training and ordered Japanese aircraft factories to experiment with fighter aircraft design. This resulted in the Zero, a devastatingly efficient fighter that had no match during the first years of the war in the Pacific.

While Japan underwent a new frenzy of battleship building in 1935, Yamamoto became chief of the navy's aviation department and was promoted to vice admiral. He continued to speak loudly about the superiority of airpower and was bewildered by Japan's obsolete battleship policy. "Battleships will be as useful to Japan in modern warfare as a samurai sword," he said.

In 1939 Yamamoto was made commander-in-chief of the combined fleet. After Japan joined Germany and Italy in the Tripartite Pact, he knew war was inevitable and dedicated himself to creating a winning strategy for the Imperial Navy. He crafted a daring, widely opposed plan to crush America's navy—a surprise attack on Pearl Harbor.

On April 18, 1943, exactly one year to the day after the Doolittle Raid on Tokyo, Yamamoto was killed when his plane was shot down by American P-38 fighters over the Solomon Islands.

ABOVE: *Actor Mako plays Yamamoto in the movie.* LEFT: *Archival photograph of Admiral Isoroku Yamamoto.*

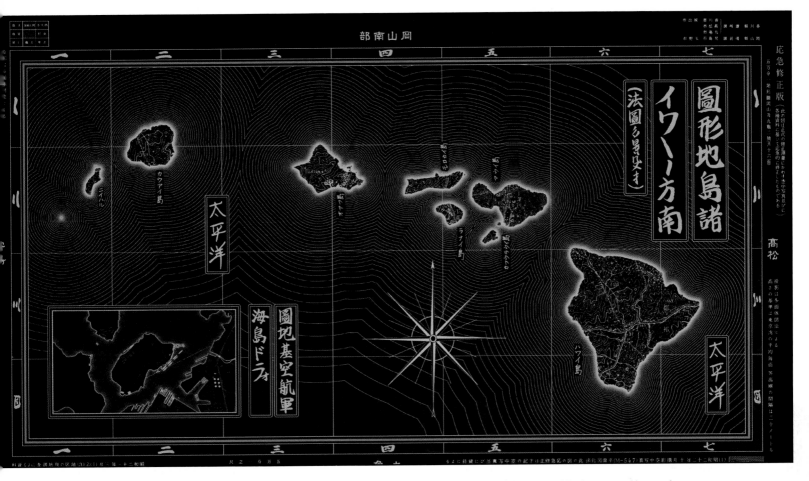

ABOVE: The Japanese map of the Hawaiian islands was created by several artists as part of the war counsel set and used as a textural reference prop for the scene (as shown below). It wasn't until after the scene was shot that Nigel Phelps discovered that in the upper right hand corner of the map, the center panel of Japanese writing was inadvertently positioned upside down.

1933. In 1937, Japan launched a new attack and seized most of the coastline of China. Throughout these bloody battles, Chinese forces never came to complete surrender, and Japan's war with China continued until 1945.

Japan further distanced itself from the United States when it signed the Three-Power Pact with Germany and Italy in 1940. The rift between Japan and the United states was widening beyond the point of no return, and to denounce Japan's aggression with China, the United States cut off all oil exports to Japan in 1941. Japan purchased nearly 80 percent of its oil supply from the United States, and this embargo gave Japan an even stronger drive to obtain oil-rich territories in Southeast Asia. With an unprecedented ship-building program underway, Japan was poised

We tried to be honest and fair on the movie. The Japanese, for example, are presented as honorable people who felt threatened by the United States. I would not have made this movie if I thought it was a piece of propaganda.

—Ben Affleck

for war. In July of 1941, it occupied French Indochina and continued to polish its plans for a massive strike against the Philippines, Hawaii and other Pacific bases.

On November 5, 1941, Japan ratified its plan of conquest in Southeast Asia. The program was outlined as follows:

1. Landings by amphibious forces at a number of different sites in the Philippines, followed by the destruction of American air power and of the naval base at Cavite. Simultaneous landings to be made on Guam, the British Malay Peninsula, Hong Kong and British North Borneo.
2. A carrier air strike to be mounted on the United States fleet at Pearl Harbor.
3. Rapid exploitation of initial success by seizing Manila . . . and Mindanao . . . Wake Island, the Bismarcks, and also Bangkok and Singapore.
4. The occupation of the Dutch East Indies (with its oil) and the continuation of the war with China.

The success of an attack on the U.S. fleet in Hawaii hinged upon two major points: the ability to obtain complete surprise and the design of torpedoes that would operate in the shallow waters of the harbor. After months of studies and tests, Admiral Yamamoto, the architect of the attack plan, was confident that his strategy successfully

YAMAMOTO: Set up teams of radio operators to send out messages the Americans will intercept, concerning every potential target in the Pacific. Include Hawaii—the clutter will be more confusing that way.

GENDA: Brilliant, Admiral.

YAMAMOTO: A brilliant man would find a way not to fight a war.

—*Randall Wallace*

THE ZERO

Light, fast, and capable of unheard-of turning, climbing and range, the Zero took the United States by complete surprise at Pearl Harbor. Before the attack, no one knew that the Japanese had developed a fighter that could outperform every other airplane in the world.

The Mitsubishi Zero-Sen was put into production in 1940; Japanese year 5700, from whence the plane got its name.

The Zero, known as "Zeke" by the Allies, was a single-seat, low-wing plane armed with two 7.7 mm machine guns and two 20-mm cannons in its wings, and two 132-pound bombs suspended below them. As a flyer, the Zero carried a 14-cylinder, 1,130-horsepower engine that drove its three-blade propeller. At top speed, the Zero flew 350 miles per hour and could fly easily at 20,000 feet, higher than any other fighters. Due to a 156-gallon internal fuel tank and 94-gallon external tank—which was dropped when empty, making the plane even more light-weight—the Zero had a range twice that of the standard U.S. fighter, the P-40.

The Zeros proved to be a major success in the skies of Pearl Harbor, but after the Battle of Midway American pilots learned how to exploit the plane's design weaknesses, such as its inability to take deep dives. They also discovered that the unarmored, fuel-filled Zero was easily ignited. Eventually, the Allies met the challenge of the

Zero with new fighter planes, the Lightnings, Corsairs, and Hellcats.

In the last stage of the war, many Zeros were converted to kamikaze planes for use in suicide missions. Over the course of the war, more than 10,400 Zeros were built.

Wreckage of a Japanese dive-bomber that was shot down over Wheeler Airfield and crashed near Wahiawa. Despite the fact that conditions for launching aircraft were tricky due to a strong southerly sea, the Japanese lost very few planes in the launching.

Derelict Japanese Naval aircraft on the Atsugi
Airfield in Japan after the surrender in 1945.
Planes include Mitsubishi A6M5 and J2M3
fighters and Nakajima Jini Recce Aircraft.
During the December 7 attack, the Japanese
lost a total of 29 planes, five midget submarines
and one 1-class submarine.

In addition to the Zero fighter planes, two types of bombers were used in the Pearl Harbor air attack. The Aichi D3A1 Type 99 dive bomber, nicknamed "Val" by the Allies, was Japan's heavy-hitting workhorse plane. It was armed with three 7.7-millimeter machine guns and carried a bomb load of more than 500 pounds. Designed for a two-man crew, the Val's appearance was distinguished by the "spats" covering its main landing gear.

In the first wave attack, Lieutenant Commander Takahashi led his unit of 51 Val dive bombers over the Pearl Harbor naval air station and Hickam and Wheeler Fields. Each plane dropped a 250-kilogram land bomb on these target areas. About two hours later, Lieutenant Commander Egusa swept in with a unit of 78 more Vals in the second wave of the attack. Each of these planes carried a 250-kilogram ordinary bomb that was dropped on targets on Ford Island and ships in the harbor.

The other bomber used at Pearl Harbor was the Nakajima B5N2 Type 97, the "Kate." This high-level bomber and torpedo plane made up the largest part of the attack air fleet. Kates carried a crew of three and were armed with

ABOVE: The USS Lexington *was propped to resemble a Japanese aircraft carrier.*
LEFT: Actor ties on a hachimaki, *the white headband symbolizing the fighter's willingness to die for Japan.*

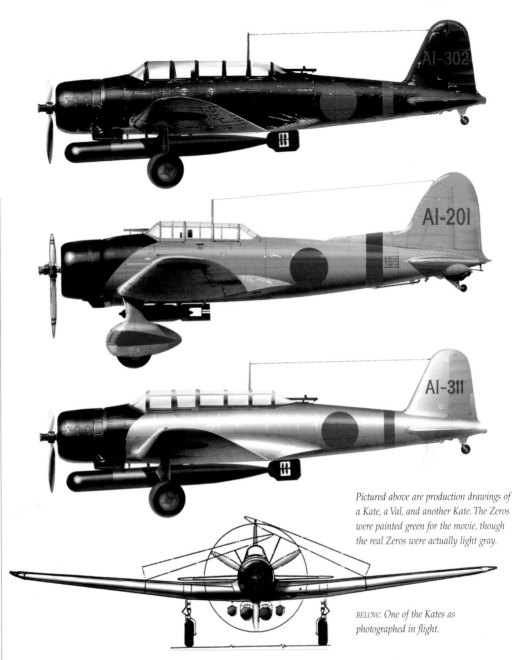

Pictured above are production drawings of a Kate, a Val, and another Kate. The Zeros were painted green for the movie, though the real Zeros were actually light gray.

BELOW: One of the Kates as photographed in flight.

either bombs or torpedoes.

In the first wave, 40 Kates, led by Lieutenant Commander Murata, flew in low to strike the eight battleships in the harbor with 800-kilogram torpedoes. Another group of 49 Kates, led by Commander Fuchida, maneuvered as a horizontal bombing unit to drop their 800-kilogram armor-piercing bombs on the ships.

During the second wave, Lieutenant Commander Shimazaki led 54 additional Kates over Hickam Field and three naval air stations. The Kates in this bombing unit carried either two 250-kilogram land bombs or one land bomb and six 60-kilogram ordinary bombs.

TORPEDOES

The Japanese worked harder and longer on torpedo design than any other nation. Naval treaties written after World War I limited the number of ships the Japanese Imperial Navy could build, so they opted to make torpedoes their equalizing weapon. The most famous result of the program was the Type 93 "Long Lance." This huge missile—30 feet long and 24 inches in diameter—traveled at 49 knots and delivered half a ton of explosive. The exceptionally fast, long-range and accurate Long Lance—launched from destroyers and cruisers—was a major force against Allied warships in the Pacific war.

The torpedoes used at Pearl

Harbor were dropped from the air, carried by the "Kate" bombers. Torpedo design was the most difficult technical challenge of Japan's Operation Hawaii. In the shallow water of Pearl Harbor (only 40 feet deep), a standard airborne torpedo would drive straight into the mud rather than straighten out and swim to its target. The Imperial Navy solved this problem by making extreme modifications to their Type 91 torpedo, a 17.7-inch model. The anti-roll stabilizing system consisted of small gyro-controlled flippers

added to each side of the torpedo. In addition, wooden frames were attached to better control the torpedo's travel through the air. Upon hitting the water, these wooden frames, as well as the missile's wooden tails, broke off. Once in the water, horizontal rudders gave the torpedo a sharp "hook" that set it upon a horizontal path.

These hardware modifications were not enough for success, however. Japan's bomber pilots had to undergo specialized training to master the precise angle and height

SECRET
WEAPONS

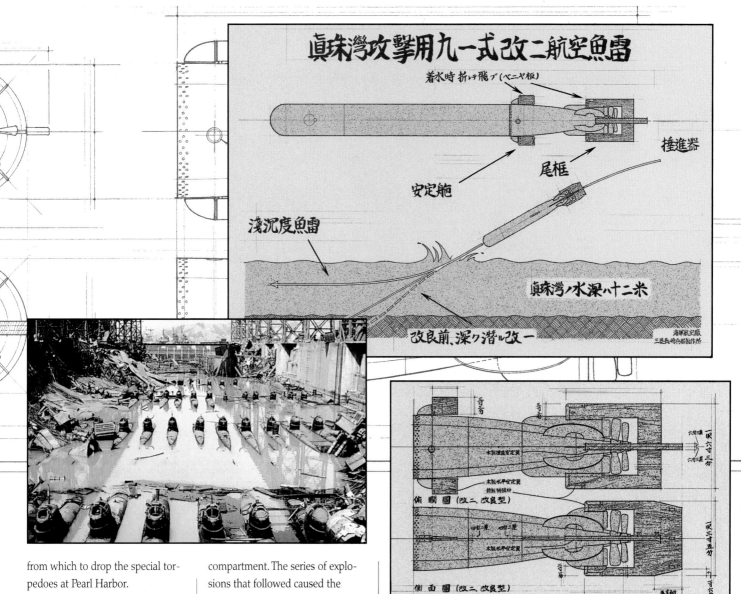

眞珠灣攻擊用九一式改二航空魚雷

着水時折レテ飛ブ（ベニヤ板）

捶進器

安定舵

尾框

淺沈度魚雷

眞珠灣ノ水深八十二米

改良前、深ク潛ル改一

海軍航空廠
三菱長崎兵器製作所

俯瞰圖（改二、改良型）

側面圖（改二、改良型）

from which to drop the special torpedoes at Pearl Harbor.

BOMBS

Another secret design of the Pearl Harbor plan was the armor-piercing bomb. This delayed-fuse bomb was outfitted with fins that propelled it through a ship's thick, protected decks. Before exploding, it penetrated into the inner compartments of a ship, thus causing much more damage than an ordinary bomb. It was this type of bomb that broke through the deck of the USS *Arizona*, igniting an explosives-filled compartment. The series of explosions that followed caused the greatest number of deaths that day.

MIDGET SUBMARINES

Designed for torpedo attacks, Japan's Type A midget submarines were 78 feet long and designed for a crew of two. Each sub had a 10-foot periscope and carried two torpedoes. Five midget subs were included in the Pearl Harbor attack force. Their orders were to slip into the harbor channel, settle to the bottom, wait for the attack and then launch their torpedoes.

One of these top-secret weapons was sited outside the harbor about an hour before the attack. It was sunk by the USS *Ward*—in firing that signaled the first shots of America's involvement in the war. Two of the remaining four midget subs were sunk during the attack, one was captured, and one has not yet been found.

ABOVE: Diagrams of Japanese torpedoes were created by Aric Lasher and Eric Rosenberg to use as backdrops for scenes where the Japanese plan their attack. The artists drew the illustrations and then sent the words to a translator to be scripted in an old Japanese writing style. Background blueprints were drawn by Aric Lasher. ABOVE LEFT: Archival image of the midget subs warehoused in Japan. FAR LEFT: The Japanese characters spell the words "Top Secret." LEFT: Scene from the movie where the Japanese prepare for their invasion aboard an aircraft carrier.

天佑ヲ確信シテ
全軍突撃セヨ

"Believe in God,
All people must attack."

PART II

DECEMBER 7, 1941

As the Japanese planned their attack throughout the months of 1941, crucial U.S. military intelligence was never passed along to Army and Navy chiefs in Hawaii. Part of the problem lay in the organization of the United States' military intelligence system itself. In spite of brilliant code-breaking successes, crucial intelligence information was not analyzed by a central office that could see a pattern emerge. Also, because of deep fears that the Japanese would discover that some of their codes had been broken, very few messages were relayed to Hawaii—the risk of interception by spies seemed too high.

By late November, diplomacy had run thin: Japan still refused to get out of China and the United States would not lift its crushing oil embargo. On the 24th, Roosevelt told his cabinet: "We are likely to be attacked next Monday for the Japs are notorious for attacking without warning." No one expected the target to be Pearl Harbor, however. For months, the Army and Navy reported with certainty that the Philippines would be the target.

We had intense meetings with the Pentagon, the secretary of defense, and many admirals and generals. We were asking for unprecedented military cooperation. We literally needed to make war on Pearl Harbor's Ford Island for six weeks with planes flying and hundreds and hundreds of stunt men and bombs going off. They basically gave us full access. I mean, full access, and kept their base going around us.

—MICHAEL BAY

On the 27th, an alert went out to all Pacific commands: "NEGOTIATIONS WITH JAPAN APPEAR TERMINATED. . . . HOSTILE ACTION POSSIBLE AT ANY MOMENT." When Admiral Kimmel received an even more specific alert, "THIS DISPATCH IS TO BE CONSIDERED A

ABOVE: *Archival aerial images of Pearl Harbor before the attack.* PREVIOUS PAGE: *Yuji Okumato plays a Japanese bomber.*

WAR WARNING . . . AGGRESSIVE ACTION EXPECTED BY JAPAN IN THE NEXT FEW DAYS," he assumed that his command in Hawaii was under no immediate threat because the report also stated that the attack was expected to hit "Philippines, Thai or Kra Peninsula or Borneo."

As a result, civilians and soldiers in Hawaii went about their usual routines on the early morning of December 7th. Planes on the airfields remained lined up to protect against sabotage and were not ready for battle. Only a fraction of the Army's anticraft gunnery throughout the island was armed or manned. No anti-torpedo nets surrounded the battleships. The radar siting of a large air group went virtually ignored, assumed to be a U.S. squadron of B-17s. And a crucial "be on alert" warning—regarding a Japanese ultimatum to be given at 8:00 A.M. Hawaii time—didn't reach General Short until 2:58 that afternoon—hours after the attack was over.

0300 HRS
As Hawaii sleeps, more than a dozen Japanese warships— aircraft carriers, battleships, cruisers and destroyers—knife southward through the sea, 300 miles north of the islands.

0342 HRS
A watchman aboard the U.S. minesweeper *Condor* sights a periscope slicing through the surface of the water about one mile outside the Pearl Harbor entrance buoys. The captain sounds general quarters, and for the next half hour the minesweeper crisscrosses the dark water but finds nothing. The captain orders the patrol destroyer *Ward* to investigate. A defective submarine net remains open in the harbor.

0550 HRS
With the Japanese attack fleet 200 miles north of Oahu, the six aircraft carriers increase their speed, turn into the wind and run up the battle flag. Japanese pilots make final preparations for launch. Two Japanese reconnaissance planes report that the U.S. fleet is docked and that "all is quiet in Pearl Harbor."

0600 HRS
On the other side of Hawaii, 200 miles south of Oahu, the U.S. aircraft carrier *Enterprise* launches 18 aircraft to scout ahead and land at Ford Island, Pearl Harbor at approximately 8:00 a.m.

0610 HRS
220 miles north of Oahu, Admiral Nagumo orders the first wave attack launch of 185 planes from six carriers. First to take off are the fighter planes, followed by heavily laden high-level bombers and, lastly, the dive-bombers and torpedo planes. Within 15 minutes, the entire first wave (minus two planes that failed to launch) is airborne, led by Commander Fuchida.

0630 HRS

The captain of the U.S. supply ship *Antares* is startled to see the conning tower of a submarine approaching the entrance to Pearl Harbor. The destroyer *Ward* is again notified of the submarine sighting and a Navy patrol plane is dispatched to the scene.

0645 HRS

The *Ward* opens fire on the target sub, hitting its conning tower, and closes in to drop depth charges. These are the first shots of the Pacific War.

0653 HRS

Captain Outerbridge of the *Ward* sends a message to the Commandant of the 14th Naval District: "We have attacked, fired upon and dropped depth charges upon submarine operating in defensive sea area."

0700 HRS

Commander Fuchida, flying toward Oahu, directs his pilots to home in on the island's local radio station.

0702 HRS

Army privates Joseph Lockhard and George Elliott at the Opana Radar Station pick up what appears to be a flight of unidentified aircraft bearing in 132 miles north of Oahu.

0710 HRS

Private Elliott phones in radar information to Fort Shafter. The only officer present at the newly established Fort Shafter Information Center is Lieutenant Kermit Tyler, who began his on-the-job-training four days earlier. Based on limited information, Tyler concludes that the radar echo must be a group of new U.S. B-17 bombers from California that are expected to land at Hickam Air Base that morning. "Don't worry about it," he tells the radarmen.

0715 HRS
Captain Outerbridge's submarine attack message, delayed in decoding, is delivered to Admiral Kimmel's duty officer. Due to the large amount of false submarine reports, Admiral Kimmel is still awaiting confirmation of the incident. North of Hawaii, the Japanese launch the second wave of 168 assault aircraft.

0735 HRS
An important message from General Marshall in Washington to Lieutenant General Short is received via Radio Corporation of America (RCA) in Honolulu. The cablegram is in an envelope labeled "Commander General" and is not identified as priority. RCA messenger Tadao Fuchikami gathers it with other deliveries and begins his route.

0735 HRS
A Japanese reconnaissance plane from the cruiser *Chikuma* reports to the attack aircraft that the main fleet is in Pearl Harbor.

0739 HRS
Opana Radar Station shows that the incoming aircraft are only 22 miles north of Oahu. Then the radar fades due to the "dead zone" caused by the surrounding hills. Minutes later, 183 Japanese planes cross the shoreline.

0753 HRS
Commander Fuchida sends out the code words "Tora! Tora! Tora!" (Tiger! Tiger! Tiger!), signaling that they have caught the enemy unaware and completely off-guard.

0755 HRS
Kanehoe Naval Air Station
Lying east of the harbor, this air patrol station is attacked by Japanese Zeros and dive bombers which quickly destroy every one of the 33 patrol planes which had been parked in neat rows out in the open to prevent sabotage.

Wheeler Air Field

Ten miles north of Pearl Harbor, Wheeler was the largest American fighter base in the Pacific. More than 100 Army Air Corps P-40s and P-36s stood along the runway. Waves of Japanese aircraft struck the planes and hangars with bombs, cannon fire and machine gun bursts.

Schofield Barracks

As Japanese dive-bombers make a strafing run over the barracks, Lieutenant Saltzman and Sergeant Klatt fire automatic rifles at the planes, bringing one of them down.

Ewa Marine Base

Two squadrons of Japanese fighters target this air station four miles west of Pearl Harbor. Flying 200 miles per hour, the crisscrossing fighters destroy more than 30 of the base's 49 fighter and scout planes parked on the ground.

Bellows Field

A single plane buzzed the field of the Army's fighter base, firing about 50 rounds. A few minutes later, nine planes appeared and shot up the field.

Hickam Field

Japanese planes bomb and strafe the Army Air Corps 2,000-acre field, the largest base on Oahu. The planes attack approximately 60 planes and the base's hangers and barracks.

Ford Island Naval Air Station

Lying within Pearl Harbor, Ford Island stationed 100 aircraft and several hangars. Lieutenant Logan Ramsey, standing in the command center, heard a plane make a low dive overhead and angrily called out for the pilot's identification. When an explosion rocked the base a few seconds later, he discovered they were under Japanese attack and immediately ordered all radiomen to send out the dispatch: "AIR RAID PEARL HARBOR THIS IS NO DRILL."

BATTLESHIP ROW

Forty torpedo planes sweep over the harbor where the majority of the United States Pacific Fleet is anchored. Within the first minutes of the attack, forty torpedoes streak the surface of the water.

The light cruiser *Helena*, moored at 1010 dock, is hit by a torpedo which cripples her and the minelayer *Oglala* moored beside her. The target ship *Utah*—anchored where the Japanese expected to find an aircraft carrier—is hit and begins to capsize. Six torpedoes strike the *West Virginia* at the center of Battleship Row. In rapid succession, five torpedoes hit the *Oklahoma* and the battleship begins to roll. Within minutes it capsizes and its superstructure pierces the mud of the harbor floor. Two torpedoes hit the *California*, and a bomb crashes through deck and explodes. On the deck of the *Nevada*, the Navy band begins playing "The Star-Spangled Banner" and the Marines begin to raise the American flag. In the near distance, they see aircraft diving at the other end of Ford Island and hear explosions. Figuring it is a practice attack, they continue to play. A Japanese plane sweeps in and drops a torpedo while its rear gunner fires at the men but only manages to shred the flag. Remarkably, the men hold their positions through the final notes of the National Anthem, then run for cover. The torpedo misses, but a second one tears into the *Nevada*'s port bow. The ship gets up steam and begins heading for the harbor entrance. Machine guns on deck open fire on torpedo planes and hit two of them. The repair ship *Vestal*, moored outboard of the battleship *Arizona*, also opens fire.

0800 HRS

B-17s from the mainland—unarmed and nearly out of fuel—reach Oahu after a 14-hour flight. Aircraft from the carrier *Enterprise* also arrive at Ford Island, and all planes are caught between enemy and friendly fire.

The planes were coming low, really low. Fast and continuous. I was surprised that none of them went down in the water. It was the loudest thing I've even been in. But it helped to get you in the mood because you felt like you were at war.

—CUBA GOODING, JR.

DORIS MILLER'S NAVY CROSS CITATION

For distinguished devotion to duty, extraordinary courage and disregard for his own personal safety during the attack on the Fleet in Pearl Harbor, Territory of Hawaii, by Japanese forces on December 7, 1941. While at the side of his Captain on the bridge, Miller, despite enemy strafing and bombing and in the face of a serious fire, assisted in moving his Captain, who had been mortally wounded, to a place of greater safety, and later manned and operated a machine gun directed at enemy Japanese attacking aircraft until ordered to leave the bridge.

ABOVE: *Cuba Gooding, Jr., and Michael Bay on location for the first day of principal photography on the movie.*

dove into the oily, flaming water. The *West Virginia* was on its way to the bottom of the harbor, struck by two armor-piercing bombs and five torpedoes. Of the 1,541 men aboard the *West Virginia* that morning, 130 were killed and 52 wounded.

The Navy's official Action Report of the attack states that "Miller . . . was instrumental in hauling people along through oil and water to the quarterdeck, thereby unquestionably saving the lives of a number of people who might otherwise have been lost." As a result, Dorie Miller was commended by Secretary of the Navy Frank Knox on April 1, 1942. On May 27 he was awarded the Navy Cross for his courage in battle during the attack on Pearl Harbor.

Admiral Chester W. Nimitz, Commander in Chief of the Pacific Fleet, personally presented the medal to Miller at a ceremony on the aircraft carrier USS *Enterprise*. Commenting on this honorable citation, Nimitz said, "This marks the first time in this conflict that such high tribute has been made in the Pacific Fleet to a member of his race and I'm sure that the future will see others similarly honored for brave acts."

The month following the Pearl Harbor attack, Miller was transferred to the USS *Indianapolis*, then assigned to the newly constructed escort carrier USS *Liscome Bay* in 1943. The War in the Pacific now turning for the allies, the *Liscome Bay* was one of five escort carriers

taking part in Operation Galvanic, an offensive maneuver in the central Pacific. In the predawn hours of November 24, 1943, the *Liscome Bay* was hit by a torpedo fired from a Japanese submarine. The torpedo explosion detonated the ship's aircraft bomb magazine, sinking the carrier within minutes. Only 272 sailors survived the sinking of the ship. Doris Miller was among the 646 who died.

The U.S. Navy honored Doris Miller once again in 1973 by commissioning a frigate ship in his name: the USS *Miller*.

THE USS *OKLAHOMA*

Among the battleships targeted for attack in Pearl Harbor was the USS *Oklahoma*, moored next to the USS *Maryland*. At 7:50 A.M., three torpedoes hit the *Oklahoma* almost simultaneously. Commander Jesse L. Kenworthy immediately gave the order to abandon ship; however, the ship was already listing at 35° and more torpedoes were on their way.

Within fifteen minutes, the battleship had been hit by five torpedoes, rolled over, and completely capsized. The antiaircraft guns and masts that once rose from her decks now pierced the mud at the bottom of the harbor.

While the *Oklahoma* was rolling, sailors tried to scramble from the oily deck onto the *Maryland*, but many were killed as Japanese planes strafed the ship. Those who did make it onto the *Maryland* stayed in the fight and helped man the antiaircraft guns.

The *Oklahoma* rolled over so quickly that many men were trapped in the capsized hull. Those inside who had not drowned or been killed by lethal fumes made their way to the hull to bang out an SOS. For the next three days, men flocked to the *Oklahoma* to help rescue the trapped survivors. One of the most successful rescues was organized by a civilian, Julio DeCastro, whose team broke through the ship and saved 32 men.

Four hundred fifteen men died on the *Oklahoma*, most of them trapped in the sunken hull.

Lt. Cmdr. Charles Coe saw the *Oklahoma* roll over and sink while he raced from his home to his headquarters during the attack. "The capsizing of the *Oklahoma* was to me a sight beyond all belief," he recalled.
"To watch this big battleship capsize . . . and to realize that U.S. officers and men were still in there—well, I just couldn't believe it. It made me realize as nothing else that war had come to Hawaii."

LEFT: *Movie still of the rollover of the USS* Oklahoma; *photographed by Jerry Bruckheimer.* INSET: *Archival image of the* Oklahoma *after the attack.*

A SURVIVOR ACCOUNT

USS Oklahoma *survivor Adolph D. Mortensen, twenty-five years old in 1941, recalls the morning of December 7, 1941.*

I was the junior officer of the boiler division of the battleship *Oklahoma.* Following late night duty, I had gone to sleep shortly after 4:00 A.M. that Sunday morning. Less than three hours later, the sound of a voice on the ship's loudspeaker, unmistakably different from the usual announcements, brought me quickly awake. "Air raid! Air raid! This is a real attack, real planes, real bombs!" crackled from the loudspeaker, followed by an obscenity. Wearing only a pajama trouser, I raced for my battle station in a boiler room, as the big ship leaped under my feet from explosions of torpedoes hitting deep in the hull. There were no lights. There was no chance of starting the engines. The order to abandon ship was passed along by voice as the ship began to list steeply.

I attempted to get to a compartment with large portholes through which I might escape, when the veteran battleship turned turtle and I was propelled into the medical dispensary, its tiled floor now the sloping ceiling.

I found myself with four other men in the dispensary with a small pocket of air trapped above the water, our only source for life.

With my feet, I found a porthole below the water. I was able to duck down into the water and turn the knobs on the port by hand. It was an eleven-inch porthole. The first two men got out quickly. The steward was hesitant and I pushed his head through and he pulled himself out. The ship's carpenter, Mr. Austin, a large man weighing over 200 pounds, knew he'd never make it through the porthole. He reached down and held the porthole open for me. I tried to take a deep breath, but the oxygen supply was about gone. As I went out, I scraped my hips squeezing through. I think that is where I lost my pajamas. Mr. Austin couldn't get out. His was the most noble and heroic act a man could perform, knowing full well that his minutes were few.

I swam the 15 to 20 feet to the oil-covered surface of the harbor. Then, I swam to ropes hanging from the ship's bottom which was still above water. Burning oil nearby sent pillars of smoke skyward. There was a deadly silence over the harbor, interspersed with violent explosions and bursts of gunfire.

As far as I can tell, I was the last man to escape from the ship without help. Cutting torches were used to try to free some of those trapped. I got away with nothing but my skin.

Following the war, Adolph Mortensen taught high school for 27 years in Oakland, California.

The rollover of the Oklahoma *was filmed at the Fox Studio in Rosarita Beach.* RIGHT: *A portion of the deck was built to rotate and then placed in a holding tank. The tank was shallow on both sides (for the filmmakers) but deep enough in the middle (about fifty feet) for the extras to safely jump off. (Photo by Jerry Bruckheimer.) The other archival photos on these pages show the ships as they appeared following the attack and were used as reference by the filmmakers.*

One of the big moments in the movie is the capsizing of the Oklahoma, which was an enormous undertaking from the standpoint of engineering, logistics, safety and cost. We had a 150-foot section of a ship that Michael wanted to roll all the way over into the water. John Frazier and his engineers designed the biggest gimbal ever made—tons and tons of steel that moved flawlessly. When a studio looks at a budget, they attack the most expensive thing and, for us, this was it. But Michael was steadfast that the rollover was going to make this movie spectacular and he was right. We thank him for hanging onto it, and not giving it up.

—JERRY BRUCKHEIMER

0812 HRS
General Short advises the entire Pacific Fleet and Washington that "Hostilities with Japan commenced with air raid on Pearl Harbor."

0815 HRS
The KGMB radio station interrupts music with a second call ordering all military personnel to report for duty. Japanese high-level bombers fly over the harbor in five V-formations and simultaneously release their bombs. One hits the *Maryland* but inflicts little damage. The *Tennessee* takes two bomb hits on two turrets.

0817 HRS
A bomb rips through the main deck of the *Arizona*, igniting fires in the explosives-filled forward compartments. All clocks and watches on the ship stop as two million pounds of powder and high explosives detonate. A glowing fireball obliterates the forward portion of the ship. Men are blown off the repair ship *Vestal* moored alongside the *Arizona*. Pearl Harbor's most devastating blow; 1,177 officers and enlisted men die in the *Arizona* blast.

0825 HRS
USS *Helm*, the first of several destroyers to clear Pearl Harbor, spots a midget submarine struggling to enter the harbor. Shots fired miss the target, the sub frees itself from the shallow reef and submerges. At Schofield Barracks, Lieutenant Stephen Saltzman and Sergeant Lowell Klatt use their rifles to shoot down an enemy plane making a strafing run on the barracks. Thick smoke covers most of Pearl Harbor. The Japanese planes depart, flying northward to rendezvous with their fleet north of the islands.

0826 HRS
The Honolulu Fire Department responds to a call for assistance from Hickam Field.

0830 HRS
Local radio stations broadcast a third call for military personnel to report to their stations. In a rush, many personnel have no time to dress and are caught in their civilian clothing.

INSET: *Archival photo shows the massive amount of smoke generated during the attack which the filmmakers would add in post-production.*

0835 HRS

The tanker *Neosho*, half loaded with high octane aviation fuel, moves clear of Battleship Row and the oil tanks on Ford Island. Damage is reported in the city. Police warn civilians to leave the streets and return to their homes.

0839 HRS

Seaplane tender *Curtiss* sights a midget sub in harbor and fires. The submarine surfaces after sustaining damage. The destroyer *Monaghan* hits the sub and drops depth charges as she passes.

0840 HRS

The first announcement of the attack airs over local radio stations: "A sporadic air attack . . . rising sun sighted on wing tips."

0850 HRS

Lieutenant Commander Shimazaki orders the Japanese to begin the second wave of the attack, sending 54 high-level bombers to Hickam Field and 81 dive-bombers to Dry Docks One and Two. They hit the battleship *Pennsylvania* and destroyers *Cassin*, *Downs* and *Shaw*.

The *Nevada* steams seaward past the burning wreckage in the harbor, inspiring everyone who sees her. Japanese Air Commander Fuchida orders his dive-bombers to attack the *Nevada*, hoping to sink it at the harbor entrance and thus block passage through the harbor for weeks. As the *Nevada* nears the Navy Yard with fires raging on board, Lieutenant Commander Thomas intentionally grounds the ship.

Light cruisers *Honolulu* and *St. Louis* also make a run for open water. The *Honolulu* is hit by a bomb and stopped, but the *St. Louis* manages to clear the harbor entrance.

At Wheeler Air Field, the second wave is met by the few American planes now in the air. First Lieutenant Sanders leads four P-36s into a formation of Japanese Zeros and downs one of them. Second Lieutenants Welch and Taylor down six enemy planes and damage three more. Second Lieutenant Danis shoots down an enemy plane, lands and refuels, and goes up to fight again.

Hundreds of wounded overwhelm the Pearl Harbor Naval Hospital, field hospitals and the USS *Solace*, the hospital ship moored in the harbor.

0900 HRS
The crew of the Dutch liner *Jagersfontein* opens up with their guns, the first allies to join the fight. Radios throughout the island crack out urgent messages: "Get off roads and stay off!" "Don't block traffic; stay at home!" "This is the real McCoy!"

0930 HRS
A bomb falls near Hawaii Governor Poindexter's home.

1000 HRS
The Japanese first wave aircraft arrive back at their carriers 190 miles north of Oahu.

1030 HRS
The Mayor's Major Disaster Council meets at city hall. Reports from local hospitals pour in listing civilian casualties.

1100 HRS
Commander Fuchida circles over Pearl Harbor to assess damage, then heads north to return to his aircraft carrier.

1115 HRS
A state of emergency is announced over the radio by Governor Poindexter.

1142 HRS
On orders of the Army, local radio stations go off the air. General Short confers with Governor Poindexter regarding martial law.

1146 HRS
Officials receive a false report—the first of many—that enemy ground troops have landed on Oahu.

1210 HRS
American planes fly north in search of the enemy but do not locate them.

1230 HRS
Honolulu police raid the Japanese embassy and find personnel burning documents. The Army orders a blackout to begin that night.

1240 HRS
The governor confers with President Roosevelt regarding martial law. Both agree it necessary that the military take over the civilian government.

1300 HRS
Commander Fuchida lands on board the carrier *Akagi*. A discussion follows with Admiral Nagumo and staff concerning launching a third wave.

1330 HRS
Signal flags on the carrier *Akagi* order the Japanese task force to withdraw. In Hawaii, the territorial director of civil defense orders blackouts every night until further notice. Governor Poindexter prepares a proclamation that will put Hawaii under martial law approximately three hours later.

1458 HRS
RCA messenger Fuchikami delivers the cablegram from Washington, which is then decoded and given to General Short. The message reads that Japan will give an ultimatum at 1:00 P.M. Washington time (8:00 A.M. Hawaii time), adding, "Just what significance the hour set may have we do not know, but be on the alert accordingly."

IN THE HOSPITAL

Ruth Erikson, who eventually became Director of the Navy Nurse Corps, recalled the morning of December 7, 1941, in the book In and Out of Harm's Way *by Capt. Doris M. Sterner:*

It was my Sunday off. I went to have breakfast in the dining room about 7:30 that morning; sitting there and chatting with some of the other girls who were off duty and then there's this drastic, terrible noise overhead. I had an eerie feeling as I dashed out the door. The telephone was ringing at the far end and [it was] the chief nurse. She said, 'Girls, get into your uniforms, this is the real thing!'

We were right across the street from the hospital so I dashed in. The first casualty came into the orthopedic dressing room at 8:25 and it was a wound in the abdomen. Well, I can still see the chief of medicine, who was on his way to go play golf that morning, but was making rounds before he left. [He] started intravenous and transfusions and his hand was shaking as he inserted the needle in the vein. And then, of course, [getting] the patients out of bed; those that were convalescing in the orthopedic ward. If you could breathe, get up, because we needed the beds. The burn cases were just streaming in from the *Nevada*, because [it] was beached just opposite the hospital. Here were patients with charred legs and arms walking to the hospital three blocks away. So we would get them as pain-free as possible and [as] quickly and then we had big fly sprays filled

"...the staff worried about another Japanese attack, kept going on chocolate bars and coffee while nursing dying men, giving morphine and whiskey, filling old vodka bottles with hot water to serve as hot-water bottles, checking vital signs, and placing basins under the thin mattresses to catch the leaking blood."

—NURSE MYRTLE WATSON,
G.I. NIGHTINGALES

with tannic acid that we sprayed the burn areas with. This was almost a continuous thing until around four o'clock that afternoon [when] Miss Arnest came along and said, 'We don't know how long this is going to be, so let's get some people off ... because we're going to have to go on night duty right early.' So I went off at four o'clock and then at eight o'clock I went back.

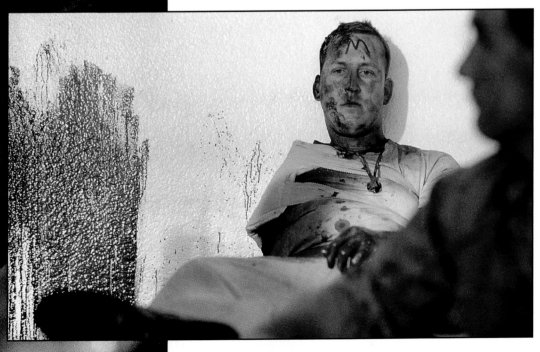

LEFT: *The number of wounded men arriving at the hospital on the morning of December 7, 1941, completely overwhelmed Pearl Harbor's small staff of doctors and nurses. Supplies were limited and to keep track of morphine disbursement, nurses used lipstick to mark an "M" on the foreheads of the men who had received a dose. This true incident was recreated in the movie.* OVERLEAF: *Pages 98–101 photos by Jerry Bruckheimer.*

EXT. PEARL HARBOR — AFTERMATH — DAY

The attack on Pearl Harbor is over—and a new human

drama has begun. The harbor is a place of shattered

bodies and shattered ships. Blood, body parts, debris

everywhere, and all of it made more hellish by

the sickening black oil fires on the water.

—*Randall Wallace*

Cutting into the *Oklahoma's* hull posed new dangers for the men trapped inside. The first two men who were located died from asphyxiation before they could be pulled out—the acetylene torch used to cut through the steel ate up the precious little oxygen in their chamber. Rescue tactics then switched to air-powered tools, which were safer but slower. This created an equally deadly problem. Air escaped from the hole more rapidly than the hole could be cut. The escaping air caused the water in the compartment to rise, endangering the men inside. Cutting teams tried to block the leaking air with rags, but they didn't always succeed in freeing the men before they drowned in the rising water.

The rescue of a group of ten men who did slip out quickly enough is described in Walter Lord's *Day of Infamy*:

> A voice yelled through the bulkhead, asking the men if they could stand a hole being drilled. Everyone shouted back yes, but it was a close thing. The air rushed out, the water surged up, and as the plate was twisted off, the men scrambled out just in time. Grinning Navy and civilian workers boosted them up . . . and they emerged into the cool, fresh air to find it was— Monday.

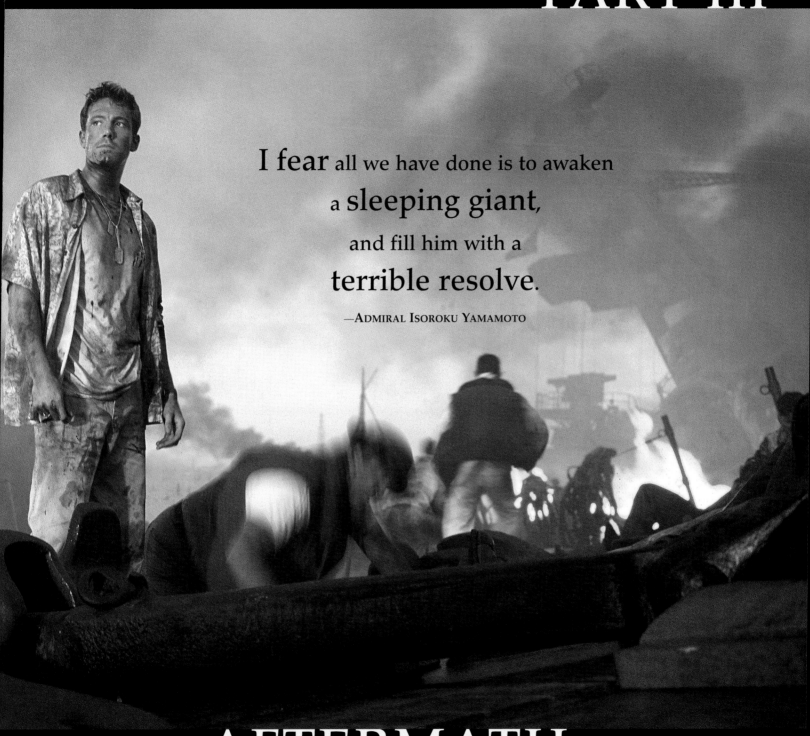

PART III

I fear all we have done is to awaken
a sleeping giant,
and fill him with a
terrible resolve.

—ADMIRAL ISOROKU YAMAMOTO

AFTERMATH

U.S. AIRCRAFT LOSSES

Hickam Field 18
Wheeler Field 53
Bellows Field 3
Ewa Marine Corps Air Station 33
Ford Island Naval Air Station 26
Kaneohe Naval Air Station 28
USS Enterprise 10
TOTAL PLANES .171

Source: U.S. Congress Joint Committee on the Pearl
Harbor Attack, 1946.

A SLEEPING GIANT

President Roosevelt was sitting in his study with his aid, Harry Hopkins, when the call came. It was Frank Knox, Secretary of the Navy, with grave news. "Mr. President," he said, "it looks like the Japanese have attacked Pearl Harbor." It was shortly after 1:30 in the afternoon; a few minutes past 8:00 a.m. Hawaii time. Hopkins refused to believe it was true, but the president figured it was all too possible that the Japanese would make a secret attack just as they were talking peace in Washington. A few minutes later, Navy Chief Admiral Harold Stark phoned to confirm the report.

Roosevelt stayed at his desk all afternoon, reading one terrible Navy Department report after another. That evening, he called his cabinet to his study, telling them this was "the most serious meeting of the cabinet that had taken place since the outbreak of the Civil War." Labor Secretary Frances Perkins, the only woman in the cabinet, recalled that the president struggled to speak and was barely able to utter the words describing the surprise attack and its devastation. "His pride in the Navy was so terrific,"

BELOW: Archival photo of the destruction of the Naval Air Station on Ford Island with a fireball in the near distance. LEFT: The movie recreates the damage done to U. S. aircraft on the ground at Wheeler and Bellows Fields.

U.S. FLEET LOSSES

USS *Arizona* . . . . Battleship . . . . . . Total Loss. Sunk. Eight heavy bomb hits.

USS *Oklahoma* . . . . . . Battleship . . . . . . Total Loss. Capsized and sunk. Five or more torpedo hits.

USS *West Virginia* . . . Battleship . . . . . . Sunk. Later raised and repaired. Five to seven
torpedo hits and two bomb hits.

USS *California* . . . . . . Battleship . . . . . . Sunk. Later raised and repaired. Two torpedo hits; one large
bomb hit and one or more bomb near misses.

USS *Nevada* . . . . Battleship . . . . . . Heavy damage. Beached and later repaired. One torpedo
hit; at least five bomb hits and two bomb near misses.

USS *Pennsylvania* . . . . Battleship . . . . . . Moderate damage. Repaired. One bomb hit.

USS *Maryland* . . . . . . Battleship . . . . . . Moderate damage. Repaired. Two bomb hits.

USS *Tennessee* . . . . . . Battleship . . . . . . Moderate damage. Repaired. Two bomb hits.

USS *Utah* . . . . Target ship . . . . . . Total Loss. Capsized and sunk. Two torpedo hits.

USS *Helena* . . . . Light cruiser . . . . Heavy damage. Repaired. One torpedo hit.

USS *Honolulu* . . . . . . Light cruiser . . . . Moderate damage. Repaired. One bomb near miss.

USS *Raleigh* . . . . Light cruiser . . . . Heavy damage. Repaired. One torpedo hit and one bomb hit.

USS *Shaw* . . . . Destroyer . . . . . . Heavy damage. Repaired. Three bomb hits.

USS *Cassin* . . . . Destroyer . . . . . . Damaged beyond repair. One direct bomb hit and secondary
explosions caused by depth charges.

USS *Downes* . . . . Destroyer . . . . . . Damaged beyond repair. Two direct bomb hits
and secondary explosions caused by depth charges.

USS *Vestal* . . . . Repair ship . . . . . Heavy damage. Repaired. Two bomb hits.

USS *Oglala* . . . . Minelayer . . . . . . Sunk. Salvaged and repaired. One torpedo passed under
the ship and exploded against the USS *Helena*.

USS *Curtiss* . . . . Seaplane tender . . Heavy damage. Repaired. One bomb hit and out-of-control
Japanese plane struck starboard crane.

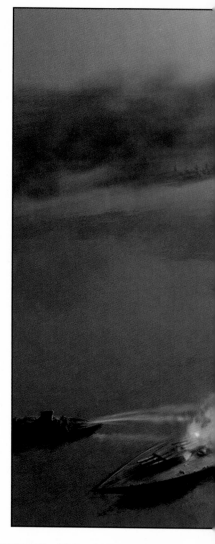

GENDA: MASTER PLANNER

In 1941, Commander Minoru Genda was the air staff officer of the Japanese Navy's first air fleet—an ace pilot with daring, original ideas about aviation and air battle. In February of that year, the thirty-six-year-old officer was handpicked for the top-secret assignment of turning Admiral Yamamoto's idea for a Pearl Harbor surprise attack into reality. "Virtually every Japanese naval officer . . . readily agreed that in 1941 Genda was the most brilliant airman in the Imperial Navy," wrote Gordon W. Prange in *At Dawn We Slept*. Commander Genda's razor-sharp intellect and breadth of knowledge about naval aviation enabled him to make Operation Hawaii a success.

After the war, Genda went on to a political career which included serving in the Japanese House of Councilors (parliament) for twenty-four years.

LEFT: *Cary Hiroyuki Tagawa, a well-known Japanese actor, plays the part of Commander Genda in the movie.*

she said, "that he was having actual physical difficulty in getting out the words that put him on record as knowing that the Navy was caught unawares."

After Roosevelt's now-legendary "Day of Infamy" speech of Monday, December 8th, both chambers approved a declaration of war against Japan. Members of the Congress were united in their sup-

ABOVE: Concept drawing by Warren Manser showing an overview of Battleship Row after the attack. RIGHT: Archival poster.

port the president's call to war on December 8, 1941. (The sole dissenting vote came from Representative Jeanette Rankin of Montana.)

News of the attack flooded the radio airwaves and evening newspapers, and by the next morning young men throughout the country formed long lines at armed forces recruiting stations. The military would eventually recruit more than 16 million volunteers and draftees.

With the declaration of war against Japan, people were put to work building ships, planes,

"It is the day we have all dreaded, yet known in our secret hearts it was our inescapable duty to meet when the world attack on freedom finally came home to us. This is the day of wrath. It is also the day of hope. . . . Either our ideals as free men shall dominate in this century, or the pitiless bayonets of our enemies will. . . . For this hour America was made."

—HENRY R. LUCE, LIFE

"Of infinitely more value than the repair of shattered ships was the welding together of the American people into a mighty spear and shield of determination. . . . The sense of outrage triggered a feeling of direct involvement which resulted in an explosion of national energy. The Japanese gave the average American a cause he could understand and believe to be worth fighting for. Thus, in a very special way Pearl Harbor became the turning point of the world struggle.

—GORDON W. PRANGE, AT DAWN WE SLEPT

ABOVE *and* OVERLEAF: *Photos by Jerry Bruckheimer.*

JAPANESE LOSSES

PERSONNEL

Airmen 55
Large I-class sub 121
Midget sub crew 9
TOTAL 185

AIRCRAFT

Fighters 9
Dive-bombers 15
Torpedo bombers 5
TOTAL 29

SUBMARINES

Large I-class subs 1
Midget subs 5
TOTAL 6

Source: *Tora! Tora! Pearl Harbor: The
Aircraft and Airmen* by Don
Thorp (Plane to Fame Pub.)

"All the News That's Fit to Print."

The New York Times.

LATE CITY EDITION
Increasing cloudiness with rising temperature today. Tomorrow cloudy, somewhat colder.
Temperatures Yesterday—Max .34; Min .25

VOL. XCI No. 30,634.

Entered as Second-Class Matter, Postoffice, New York, N. Y.

NEW YORK, MONDAY, DECEMBER 8, 1941.

Copyright, 1941, by The New York Times Company.

THREE CENTS NEW YORK and Vicinity

JAPAN WARS ON U. S. AND BRITAIN; MAKES SUDDEN ATTACK ON HAWAII HEAVY FIGHTING AT SEA REPORTED

CONGRESS DECIDED

Roosevelt Will Address It Today and Find It Ready to Vote War

CONFERENCE IS HELD

Legislative Leaders and Cabinet in Sober White House Talk

By C. P. TRUSSELL
Special to THE NEW YORK TIMES.

WASHINGTON, Dec. 7—President Roosevelt will address a joint session of Congress tomorrow and will find the membership in a mood to vote any steps he asks in connection with the developments in the Pacific.

The President will appear personally at 12:30 P. M. Whether he would call for a flat declaration of war again Japan was left unannounced tonight. But leaders of Congress, shocked and angered by the Japanese attacks, were talking of a declaration of war not only Japan but on the entire Axis.

The plans for action tomorrow were made tonight in a White House conference at which the President, surrounded by his Cabinet and by Congressional leaders of both parties, went through reports, some official, some unconfirmed, of the continued assaults of the Japanese outposts upon American Pacific outposts.

Meet Far Into Night

The conference lasted until after 11 o'clock and at its close an official statement was issued. This said that the President had reviewed at his conferees the latest advices from the Pacific and declared:

"It should be emphasized that the message to Congress has not yet been written and its tenor will, of course, depend on further information received between 11 o'clock tonight and noon tomorrow. Further news is coming in all the time."

Congressional leaders asserted as they left the White House that they did not know what the President would say tomorrow.

"Will the President ask for a declaration of war?" Speaker Rayburn was asked.

"He didn't say," answered the Speaker.

Asked whether Congress would support a declaration of war, Mr. Rayburn observed:

"I think that is one thing on which there would be unity."

Politics Declared Dropped

"There is no politics here," said Representative Joseph W. Martin Jr., the Minority House Leader. "There is only one party when it comes to the integrity and honor of the country."

"The Republicans," said Senator Charles L. McNary of Oregon, the Senate minority leader, "will all go along, in my opinion, with whatever is asked.

Unless international develop-

TOKYO ACTS FIRST

Declaration Follows Air and Sea Attacks on U. S. and Britain

TOGO CALLS ENVOYS

After Fighting Is On, Grew Gets Japan's Reply to Hull Note of Nov. 26

By The Associated Press.

TOKYO, Monday, Dec. 8—Japan went to war against the United States and Britain today with air and sea attacks against Hawaii, followed by a formal declaration of hostilities.

Japanese Imperial headquarters announced at 6 A. M. [4 P. M. Sunday, Eastern standard time] that a state of war existed among these nations in the Western Pacific, as of dawn.

Soon afterward, Domei, the Japanese official news agency, announced that "naval operations are progressing off Hawaii, with at least one Japanese aircraft carrier in action against Pearl Harbor," the American naval base in the islands.

Japanese bombers were declared to have raided Honolulu at 7:35 A. M., Hawaii time [1:05 Sunday, Eastern standard time].

Premier-War Minister General Hideki Tojo held a twenty-minute Cabinet session at his official residence at 7 A. M.

Soon afterward it was announced that both the United States Ambassador, Joseph C. Grew, and the British Ambassador, Sir Robert Leslie Craigie, had been summoned by Foreign Minister Shigenori Togo.

The Foreign Minister, Domei said, handed to Mr. Grew the Japanese Government's formal reply to the note sent to Japan by United States Secretary of State Cordell Hull on Nov. 26.

[In the course of the diplomatic negotiations leading up to yesterday's events, the Domei agency had stated that Japan could not accept the premises of Mr. Hull's note.]

Sir Robert was summoned by

Continued on Page Five

JAPANESE FORCE LANDS IN MALAYA

First Attempt Is Repulsed—Singapore Is Bombed and Thailand Invaded

By The Associated Press.

SINGAPORE, Monday, Dec. 8—The Japanese landed in Northern Malaya, 300 miles north of Singapore, today and bombed this great British naval stronghold, causing small loss of life among civilians and property damage.

About 300 Japanese troops landed on the east coast of Malaya and began filtering through jungle-fringed swamps and rice fields toward Kota Bahru airdrome, which is ten miles from the northern terminus of a railroad leading to Singapore.

An official report from the

Continued on Page Two

The International Situation

MONDAY, DEC. 8, 1941

Yesterday morning Japan attacked the United States at several points in the Pacific. President Roosevelt ordered United States forces into action and a declaration of war is expected this morning. [Page 1, Columns 7 and 8.] Tokyo made its declaration as of this morning against both the United States and Britain. [Page 1, Column 2.] The first Japanese assault was in Hawaii. Many casualties and severe damage resulted. [Page 1, Columns 4 and 5; Map

while the President gave out the text of his fruitless appeal to the Japanese Emperor. [Page 12.] The White House was the hub of Washington activity and news bulletins were released there. [Page 12, Column 3.]

The Federal Bureau of Investigation was ordered to begin a round-up of some Japanese in this country. [Page 6, Column 8.] As New York City went on a war footing and public precautions were taken, the FBI began the detention of Japanese nationals. [Page 1, Column 4.]

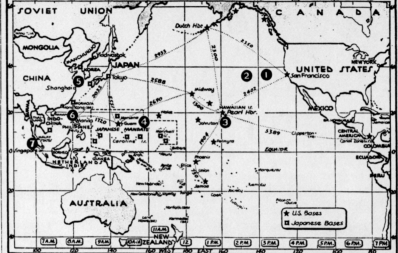

PACIFIC OCEAN: THEATRE OF WAR INVOLVING UNITED STATES AND ITS ALLIES

★ U.S. Bases
□ Japanese Bases

Shortly after the outbreak of hostilities an American ship sent a distress call from (1) and a United States Army transport carrying lumber was torpedoed at (2). The most important action was at Hawaii (3), where Japanese planes bombed the great Pearl Harbor base. Also attacked was Guam (4). From Manila (6) United States bombers roared northward, while some parts of the Philippines were raided, as was Hong Kong. At Shanghai (5) a British gunboat was sunk and an American gunboat seized. To the south, in the Malaya area (7), the British bombed Japanese ships, Tokyo forces attempted landings on British territory and Singapore underwent an air raid. Distances between key Pacific points are shown on the map in statute miles.

Tokyo Bombers Strike Hard At Our Main Bases on Oahu

By The United Press.

HONOLULU, Dec. 7—War broke with lightning suddenness in the Pacific today when waves of Japanese bombers attacked Hawaii this morning and the United States Fleet struck back with a thunder of big naval rifles. Japanese bombers, including four-engined dive bombers and torpedo-carrying planes, blasted at Pearl Harbor, the great United States naval base, the city of Honolulu and several outlying American military bases on the Island of Oahu. There were casualties of unstated number.

[The United States battleship Oklahoma was set afire by the Japanese attackers, according to a National Broadcasting Company observer, who also reported in a broadcast yesterday that two other ships in Pearl Harbor were attacked.

[The Japanese news agency, Domei, reported that the battleship Oklahoma had been sunk at Pearl Harbor, according to an United Press dispatch from Shanghai.]

[Governor Joseph B. Poindexter of Hawaii talked with President Roosevelt late yesterday afternoon, saying that a second wave of Japanese bombers was just coming over, and the Gov-

Continued on Page Thirteen

ENTIRE CITY PUT ON WAR FOOTING

Japanese Rounded Up by FBI, Sent to Ellis Island—Vital Services Are Guarded

The metropolitan district reacted swiftly yesterday to the Japanese attack in the Pacific. All large communities in the area, including New York City, Newark, Jersey City, Bayonne and Paterson, went on immediate war footing.

One of the first steps taken here last night was a round-up of Japanese nationals by special agents of the Federal Bureau of Investigation, reinforced by squads of city detectives acting under FBI supervision. More than 100 FBI men, fully armed, were assigned to the detail.

The prisoners were sent to Ellis Island, where they will be held pending action at Washington. It was indicated hundreds would be detained.

Earlier Mayor La Guardia had convened his Emergency Board and directed that Japanese nationals be confined to their homes pending the

HULL DENOUNCES TOKYO 'INFAMY'

Brands Japan 'Fraudulent' in Preparing Attack While Carrying On Parleys

Texts of Secretary Hull's note and Japan's reply, Page 10.

By BERTRAM D. HULEN
Special to THE NEW YORK TIMES.

WASHINGTON, Dec. 7—Japan was accused by Secretary of State Cordell Hull today of making a "treacherous and utterly unprovoked attack" upon the United States and of having been "infamously false and fraudulent" by preparing for the attack while conducting diplomatic negotiations with the professed desire of maintaining peace.

But even before he knew of the attack, Mr. Hull had vehemently brought the diplomatic negotiations to a virtual end with an outburst against Admiral Kichisaburo Nomura, the Japanese Ambassador, and Saburo Kurusu, special envoy, because of the insulting character of the reply they deliv-

Continued on Page Eleven

GUAM BOMBED; ARMY SHIP IS SUNK

U. S. Fliers Head North From Manila

Battleship Oklahoma Set Afire by Torpedo Planes at Honolulu

104 SOLDIERS KILLED AT FIELD IN HAWAII

President Fears 'Very Heavy Losses' on Oahu

Churchill Notifies Japan That a State of War Exists

By FRANK L. KLUCKHOHN
Special to THE NEW YORK TIMES.

WASHINGTON, Monday, Dec. 8—Sudden and unexpected attacks on Pearl Harbor, Honolulu, and other United States possessions in the Pacific early yesterday by the Japanese air force and navy plunged the United States and Japan into war.

The initial attack in Hawaii, apparently launched by torpedo-carrying bombers and submarines, caused widespread damage and death. It was quickly followed by others. There were unconfirmed reports that German raiders participated in the attack.

Guam also was assaulted from the air, as were Davao, island of Mindanao, and Camp John Hay, in Northern Luzon, both in the Philippines. Lieut. Gen. Douglas MacArthur, commanding the United States Army of the Far East, reported that there was little damage, however.

[Japanese parachute troops had been landed in the Philippines and native Japanese had seized some communities, Lieut. Gen. Arch Gunnison said in a broadcast from Manila today to WOR and Mutual. He reported without detail that "in the naval battle the ABCD fleets under American command appeared to be successful" against Japanese invasions.]

Japanese submarines, ranging out over the Pacific, sank an American transport carrying lumber 1,300 miles from San Francisco, and distress signals were heard from a freighter 700 from that city.

The War Department reported that 104 soldiers died and were wounded as a result of the attack on Hickam Field. The National Broadcasting Company reported from Honolulu that the battleship Oklahoma was afire. [Domei, Japanese news agency, reported the Oklahoma sunk.]

Nation Placed on Full War Basis

The news of these surprise attacks fell like a bombshell on Washington. President Roosevelt immediately ordered the Army and the Navy onto a full war footing. He arranged at a White House conference last night to address a joint session of Congress at noon today, presumably to ask for declaration of a formal state of war.

This was disclosed after a long special Cabinet meeting was joined later by Congressional leaders. These leaders promised "action" within a day.

After leaving the White House conference Attorney General Francis Biddle said that "a resolution" would be introduced in Congress tomorrow. He would not amplify or affirm that it was for a declaration of war.

Congress probably will "act" within the day, and the Senate Foreign Relations Committee for this purpose, Chairman Tom Connally announced.

[A United Press dispatch from London this morning said that Prime Minister Churchill had notified Japan that a state of war existed.]

As the reports of heavy fighting flashed into the White House, London reported semi-officially that the British Empire would carry out Prime Minister Winston Churchill's pledge to give the United States full support in case of hostilities with Japan. The President and Mr. Churchill talked by transatlantic telephone.

This was followed by a statement in London from the Netherland Government in Exile that it considered a state of war to exist between the Netherlands and Japan. Canada, Australia and Costa Rica took similar action.

Landing Made in Malaya

A Singapore communique disclosed that Japanese

Lewis Wins Captive Mine Fight; Arbitrators Grant Union Shop

The three-man arbitration board appointed by President Roosevelt to arbitrate the union shop dispute in the captive coal mines last night reversed the decision of the National-

surances before the decision was reached that they would accept it as binding.

The arbitration award ended a

THE DAY OF INFAMY

TOKYO, Monday, Dec. 8—Japan went to war against the United States and Britain today with air and sea attacks against Hawaii, followed by a formal declaration of hostilities.

Japanese Imperial headquarters announced at 6 A.M.. (4 P.M. Sunday, Eastern standard time) that a state of war existed among these nations in the Western Pacific, as of dawn.

Nation Placed on Full War Basis
The news of these surprise attacks fell like a bombshell on Washington. President Roosevelt immediately ordered the country and the Army and Navy onto a full war footing.

—The *New York Times*,
December 8, 1941

"For months now, the knowledge that something of this kind might happen has been hanging over our heads. . . That is all over now and there is no more uncertainty. We know what we have to face and we know we are ready to face it. . . Whatever is asked of us, I am sure we can accomplish it; we are the free and unconquerable people of the U.S.A."

—*ELEANOR ROOSEVELT RADIO ADDRESS, DECEMBER 8, 1941*

*A*s with all great men, FDR had many detractors. There's no question of his greatness—just listen to his voice from his fireside chats.

As for the rumors that he knew about the attack before it happened, I have researched this thoroughly and I can say surely that he had no knowledge of it whatsoever. Thank God we have the great documentarians. In one documentary, there is the report of his butler who was there when FDR got the news about the attack. He reported that FDR turned white and started shaking. He put his head in his hands and said, "My God, my God."

According to Eleanor Roosevelt, FDR never got over the deception of the Japanese who were negotiating peace at the hour of Pearl Harbor. He was angry about that for the rest of his life.

—JON VOIGHT

ABOVE LEFT: Early edition of the Honolulu Star-Bulletin *reported 6 dead and 21 injured in the attack. FAR LEFT: Headlines in* The New York Times *reported 104 dead. TOP RIGHT: Michael Bay directs Jon Voight for his "Day of Infamy" speech scene. ABOVE: FDR in a formal portrait.*

DOOLITTLE: We might have lost this battle. But we're gonna win this war. You know how I know? There's just nothing stronger than the heart of a volunteer.

—Randall Wallace

THE DOOLITTLE RAID

Two weeks after the attack on Pearl Harbor, President Roosevelt gathered his military leaders at the White House to discuss how to strike back at the Japanese. Roosevelt was emphatic about working out a plan for a bombing raid on Japan that would bring the war to their home islands and bolster American morale. A bomb strike on military sites in Tokyo and other targets would crush the view that Japan was invulnerable to attack, an attitude that had permeated Japanese consciousness for more than 700 years. It would bring a much-needed win to the American battle score in the Pacific, which was at an all-time low in the spring of 1942. Three of those present at the White House meeting were General George C. Marshall, Army chief of staff; General Henry H. "Hap" Arnold, chief of staff of the Army Air Corps; and Admiral Ernest J. King, chief of naval operations.

In the weeks just after the attack, Roosevelt also held meetings with Prime Minister Winston Churchill and other leaders to outline an overall strategy for the War. One of these meetings focused on an attack plan for North Africa. Admiral King made a suggestion about using heavy bombers launched from aircraft carriers rather than ground air-strips for these missions. In his notes from that meeting, King wrote: "We will have to try bomber takeoffs from carriers. It has never been done before but we must try it out and check on how long it takes." The idea presented many problems. How could a bomber, which is a much larger and heavier plane than a fighter aircraft, take off from a carrier deck loaded down with bombs, gas and crew? General Arnold's War Plans Division took on the task of studying the possibility.

A few days after that meeting, the same idea—as a plan for bombing Japan—occurred to Captain Francis S. Low, a submariner and operations officer on Admiral King's staff. At the Norfolk, Virginia, Naval Air Station, Captain Low saw the outline of a carrier deck painted on an airfield. Army bomber pilots were making practice runs over the simulated carrier. Low connected the idea of bombers and carriers, and figured that because bombers have a longer range than fighters, they could be launched farther out at sea and possibly make a surprise attack. The captain went to Admiral King with his idea. The Admiral sent Low to Captain Donald Duncan, the air operations manager, who began an in-depth study of launching bombers from carriers. His 30-page handwritten report (he wouldn't entrust top-secret material to a typist), concluded that the

I asked one of the original Doolittle Raiders, "So what was it like on the carrier, when you were first told that you were on your way to bomb Tokyo?" He said, "Well, I remember asking my friend, 'Do you think they picked us just 'cause we're young and dumb?'" We used that line in the movie, even though these guys weren't dumb. Quite the opposite—they were chosen for their intelligence and skill; they were some of our best pilots and technicians, and they were supremely dedicated fliers.

—MICHAEL BAY

American B-25 bomber could be modified to do the job. But huge obstacles had to be overcome in takeoff speed and range, fuel storage, and pilot training.

Admiral King and General Hap Arnold agreed that a carrier-based mission was the only way to make the bombing operational. The Army was already working on the technical aspects of outfitting bombers for carriers. Although a

After Pearl Harbor, we were defeated in the Philippines. The Japanese were marching across China, the Marshall Islands, the Solomons and we were losing every battle. Every day you opened the newspaper and it was more bad news about American boys getting killed. The only thing that changed that mood in this country and gave us hope was Jimmy Doolittle's raid on Tokyo.

—JERRY BRUCKHEIMER

land-based mission would be much easier, the United States could not get permission from China or the Soviet Union to use their airfields. Chiang Kai-shek feared how the Japanese, who occupied Manchuria, would retaliate against his people, and the Soviet Union was taking a neutral stance in regard to Japan.

To be successful, the Tokyo mission would need the leadership of someone who knew piloting, planes and engineering and who wasn't afraid of tackling the impossible. "Get me Doolittle!" General Hap Arnold barked to his assistant over the phone on January 17, 1942. Next to Charles Lindbergh and Eddie Rickenbacker, Lieutenant Colonel James Harold Doolittle was the most famous flyer in America. A daredevil flyer, world-famous racer and pioneer of instrument flying, Doolittle had been a flight instructor in World War I and held a doctorate in aeronautics from the Massachusetts Institute of Technology, which earned him the title "Dr. Doolittle."

Doolitte was born in Alameda, California, in 1886, but at the age of four moved with his family to Nome, Alaska, where his father hoped to cash in on the gold rush. A small boy with long, angelic curls, Jimmy quickly learned how to take care of himself in a rough, muddy town like Nome. Back in California at age 15, he'd become the amateur flyweight championship of the West

Coast. He would need this hardiness the rest of his life because, at 5 feet 4 inches tall and 140 pounds, Doolittle often had to battle to have his orders and ideas taken seriously.

Before finishing his degree in mining engineering at Berkeley, Doolittle enlisted in the Army and learned how to fly. Much to his displeasure, he never saw combat. The Army used him as a flight instructor throughout the war and then sent him to MIT, where he received one of the first degrees in aeronautical science. As an Army pilot, Doolittle broke many records, including being the first pilot to fly solo coast-

Do More for Doolittle

to-coast in less than 24 hours (1922); the first pilot to break the world seaplane speed record (twice in 1925), and the first pilot in history to fly "blind," using only a radio, an artificial horizon, an altimeter and a gyrocompass (1929).

In 1930, with a wife and two sons to support, Doolittle quit the Air Corps and joined the corporate world as a member of Shell Oil Company's new aviation department in St. Louis. In addition to this job, he was hired from time to time by aircraft manufacturers to showcase new airplanes in Europe, where he kept apprised of the latest aviation developments. Upon his return from one trip, he argued the case for Shell to produce a higher-octane aviation gasoline. Doolittle knew that this would have a major impact on American aviation, especially during a war, and persevered until he was successful. It wasn't an easy fight. "That's when I learned the advantages of an advanced degree," wrote Doolittle in his autobiography. "I am sure that Jimmy Doolittle the stunt pilot and Jimmy Doolittle the racing pilot would not have been able to influ-

ence them. But I went to them as Dr. Doolittle."

When Hitler marched into Czechoslovakia in 1938, Doolittle returned to military service. Instead of getting the combat duty he requested, Doolittle started out helping Detroit retool their auto production lines for airplanes and eventually got promoted to lieutenant colonel with a Washington desk job in General Arnold's office. A month after taking this post, he received the call from Arnold and began working on the Tokyo mission. This time he would not settle for anything less than full involvement, including flying the mission himself over Tokyo. After much deliberation, he got his request. Captain Doolittle wrote up the plan and had less than three months to prepare every pilot, every plane and every maneuver. In a memo to General Arnold, he outlined the purpose and details of the "B-25 Special Project," which included the following statements:

- The purpose of this special project is to bomb and fire the industrial center of Japan.
- It is anticipated that this not only will cause confusion and impede production but will undoubtedly facilitate operation against Japan in other theaters due to their probable withdrawal of troops for

LEFT: *Archival poster of the real Jimmy Doolittle.* ABOVE: *Movie still of a B-25 bomber in the hangar.* BELOW: *Concept drawings of the bomber showing views of both the top and bottom of the plane.*

the purpose of defending the home country.

- The method contemplated is to bring carrier-borne bombers to within 400 to 500 miles of the coast of Japan, preferably to the south-southeast. They will then take off from the carrier deck and proceed directly to selected targets in the Tokyo-Yokohama, Nagoya, and Osaka-Kobe areas.
- After dropping their bombs . . . a course will be set for one or more of the following airports in

China: Chuchow, Chuchow (Lishui), Yushan, and/or Chienou.

- After refueling, the airplanes will proceed to the strong Chinese air base at Chungking, about 800 miles distant.

Doolittle assembled a group of Army engineers, navigators, pilots, gunners, radiomen and mechanics at a field near what is now Eglin Air Force Base, in Florida, to revamp 18 bombers for the mission. No one

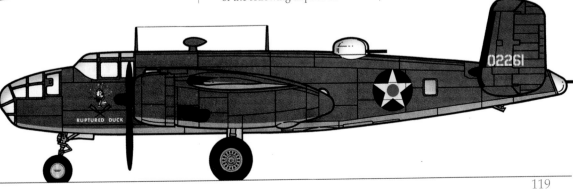

but Doolittle, however, knew the target of the top-secret mission. The crew would not discover their destination until the carrier force was out to sea headed for Japan.

Changes to the B-25s included adding two gas tanks and getting rid of all unnecessary equipment such as the top-secret and complex Norden bombsight. No one wanted to risk the Norden getting into enemy hands, and it did not work well at the low-level ranges this mission would require. In the machine shop, Captain Ross Greening designed a simple site made of aluminum that had high accuracy and added practically no weight to the plane. Captain Greening also solved the problem of having no tail guns installed in the B-25. He suggested putting two broomsticks in the back and painting them black to simulate the real thing—and hopefully deter attacks from the rear. Doolittle thought it was a great idea and ordered it done. Doolittle also ordered that the lower turret guns be removed because they were heavy and very difficult to operate. "I thought a man could learn to pay the violin well enough for Carnegie Hall before he could learn to fire that thing," he wrote.

With precious few weeks to work, the schedule at the base was tight and well organized. Engineers tossed out everything they could to

trim the B-25s as much as possible, including long-range radio transmitters. The planes had to be made light enough the take off carrying a crew of five, three additional fuel tanks and ten five-gallon cans of gasoline. Gunners were trained in .50 caliber machine gun turrets that, due to faulty manufacturing, didn't always work. Pilots were trained in making short-field takeoffs on a field marked with flags where the end of the aircraft carrier would be. Navigators honed their skills in night navigation exercises.

Doolittle worked with manufacturers to design and quickly provide specially designed parts and incendiary bombs. Rushing between manufacturing sites, Florida and Washington, Doolittle was under incredible pressure to fulfill the mission and maintain total secrecy. A mission this dangerous needed a medical doctor, but weight was such a factor that Doolittle couldn't add one more crew member to any of the planes. Flight surgeon Lieutenant Thomas R. White volunteered to train as a gunner, which would make him one of the regular crew. He learned the job so well he scored second-highest among everyone in the qualifying tests.

When the operation was shifted to California for final repairs, Doolittle met with a new crew of personnel who didn't know enough

about the mission to take his orders seriously or work at top speed. Time and again he met resistance, and time and again he had to pull rank to get things done. After one call to the base from General Arnold, however, the situation turned around and Doolittle immediately got the cooperation he needed.

Doolittle's task force, set to sail from Alameda on April 2, consisted of the aircraft carrier USS *Hornet*, two cruisers, four destroyers and an oiler ship. They would meet up in the Pacific with a second, Hawaii-based task force led by Admiral Halsey. This task force was made up of the carrier USS *Enterprise*, two cruisers, four destroyers and an

oiler. Together, the two sets of ships were called "Task Force Mike." Each B-25 would carry a five-man crew—pilot, copilot, bombardier, navigator and gunner. The mission plan was deceptively simple: fifteen bombers would take off from the *Hornet* 450 miles from Japan, come in low and drop four bombs apiece, then head south and west for landing in China. Radio homing beacons would direct the planes to airstrips in a valley near Chuchow. In the event that they did not reach the airfield, the planes would ditch in the water near the coast or crews would bail out over land.

Just before noon on April 2, the USS *Hornet* sailed into the

Pacific with 16 B-25s lashed to her deck. Once out of sight of land, the Hornet's captain felt it was safe to tell the crew where they were going. He announced through the loudspeaker, "This force is bound for Tokyo," and cheers went up throughout the ship.

On April 13, Doolittle's task force met up with Admiral Halsey's ships, and all 16 vessels steamed due west toward Japan. Originally, one of the sixteen bombers was to take off early in the voyage and fly home to show the pilots that it could be done and to muster everyone's confidence in the mission. Doolittle decided to keep the pilot, crew and plane for the mission,

however, and the practice takeoff was not made. During the long days at sea, Doolittle finalized the targets that the bombers would hit: military structures such as war industries, shipbuilding facilities and power plants. He strongly reiterated that no hospitals, schools or other civilian targets were allowed, and got very angry when hearing that some crewmen wanted to hit the Imperial Palace. "There is nothing that would unite the Japanese nation more than to bomb the emperor's home," he told them.

According to the plan, Doolittle would take off in his B-25 on the afternoon of April 19, and the rest of the planes would follow

at dusk. At 3:00 A.M. on the 18, however, radar detected two enemy ships about 21,000 yards away. The combined task force took evasive maneuvers, but at dawn they spotted another boat about 12,000 yards away. Halsey ordered the *Nashville* to sink the small vessel. Unknown to the Americans, the Japanese had set up a line of patrols about 700 miles out into the Pacific. To avoid an enemy alert, Halsey decided to launch the mission immediately. Within minutes, the *Hornet's* announcement speakers blared: "Army pilots, man your planes!" Two hundred miles farther from Tokyo than planned, the planes would barely have enough fuel to make it to the Chinese coastline. The bombing run would now take place in broad daylight. Much of the carefully designed plan was scrapped.

Doolittle, first in line to take off, lifted from the *Hornet* at 8:20 A.M. In spite of high winds, rains that drenched the deck crew and

The guy who was Doolittle's navigator and his co-pilot were with us on the aircraft carrier in Texas. They were watching Alec and these guys play Doolittle and his co-pilots and navigators.

—JOSH HARTNETT

30-foot swells that moved the carrier up and down like a teeter-totter, all 16 planes launched successfully. The weather cleared as the planes neared Japan, and at 12:30 P.M. Tokyo time Doolittle dropped all four bombs over his factory targets. Scattered by headwinds and variances in their magnetic compasses, the other fifteen planes came in from all directions over Tokyo, Yokohama, Yokosuka and Nagoya. The bombers skimmed over treetops, then gunned up to about a thousand feet and dropped their five-hundred-pound bombs. By a bizarre coincidence, Tokyo was in the final minutes of a city-wide air raid drill. Throughout the first few minutes of the bombing run, civilians and military personnel alike assumed the low-flying planes were part of the drill. Antiaircraft fire pelted the air and a few Japanese fighter planes made chase, but none of the B-25s were damaged or shot down. The combined elements of fair weather, low altitude, careful study of target maps and flying in daylight made the bombing runs accurate and successful, and each plane headed south and west over the China Sea. Crew Number Eight, however, had experienced engine problems from the start, and Captain Edward York knew they didn't have enough fuel to fly another 1,200 miles to China. Rather than land in Japan or crash

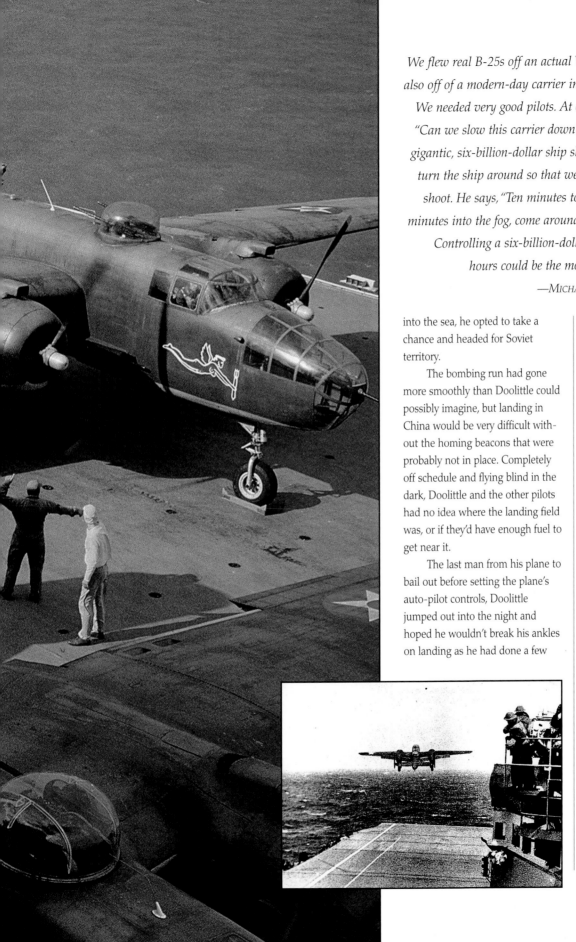

We flew real B-25s off an actual World War Two–era carrier, and also off of a modern-day carrier in actual use. It was a little tricky. We needed very good pilots. At one point I said to the captain, "Can we slow this carrier down?" And thirty seconds later this gigantic, six-billion-dollar ship slows down. Then I asked him to turn the ship around so that we could catch some good sun to shoot. He says, "Ten minutes to go one-eighty." So we go ten minutes into the fog, come around, and then we're ready to shoot. Controlling a six-billion-dollar aircraft carrier for three hours could be the most fun I've ever had.

—MICHAEL BAY

into the sea, he opted to take a chance and headed for Soviet territory.

The bombing run had gone more smoothly than Doolittle could possibly imagine, but landing in China would be very difficult without the homing beacons that were probably not in place. Completely off schedule and flying blind in the dark, Doolittle and the other pilots had no idea where the landing field was, or if they'd have enough fuel to get near it.

The last man from his plane to bail out before setting the plane's auto-pilot controls, Doolittle jumped out into the night and hoped he wouldn't break his ankles on landing as he had done a few

years previously. His landing was soft—but not pleasant. He found himself in a wet rice paddy, sinking in foul-smelling "fertilizer."

Anxious about the rest of his men and troubled over the fact that all of the planes had probably crashed, Doolittle was depressed over the outcome of the raid. "I never felt lower in my life," he wrote. One of the significant points of the mission was to deliver the B-25s to airfields in India where they would join the Allied fleet. Losing the planes was disappointing, but not knowing the whereabouts or status of his men was worse. The next day he found a Chinese military official who helped him locate his crew, and eventually everyone except the crew who flew into the Soviet Union was accounted for.

Considering the odds, the majority of Doolittle's men fared well in the landings, but there were casualties. Sergeant William Dieter and Donald Fitzmaurice drowned

FAR LEFT: *Movie still re-creating Doolittle's bombers on an aircraft carrier in the Pacific.* NEAR LEFT: *Archival photo of the real Jimmy Doolittle taking off for Toyko on April 18, 1942.*

This movie should have taken double the time in terms of shooting. People will be amazed that we only spent 100 days shooting—and ten of those were second-unit days. We basically had 90 first-unit days. We maintained an unrelenting pace. I learned from those old, wise directors that you set your pace the first week, and that's what we did. The crew was ready for it, and we'd also prepped extensively. A big help was the animatic process that I initiated four weeks after we started developing the movie's storyline. We worked with a satellite image of Pearl Harbor and digitally created the battleships and the planes. These were just crude little cartoons, but the planes could actually fly around the base, and I could create these huge, moving, epic shots in my office with just a few guys. I could literally envision a massive shot in my head at night, and see it realized on a screen the next day.   —MICHAEL BAY

ABOVE: *Two stills from the animatic Michael Bay created to show how the Doolittle Raid would be filmed.* RIGHT: *Storyboards by Robert Consing are drawn in gray and then xeroxed in blue. These boards portray the Doolittle Raid.*

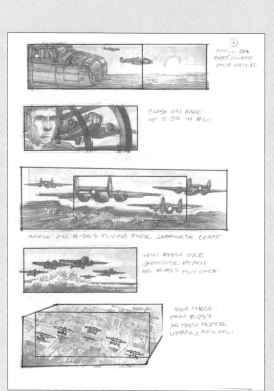

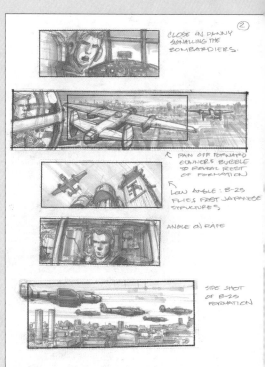

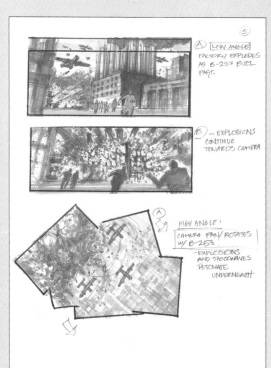

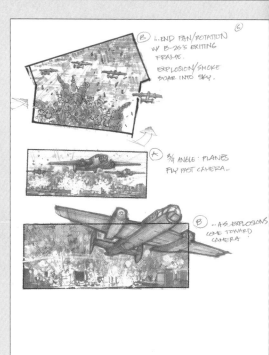

STORYBOARDS

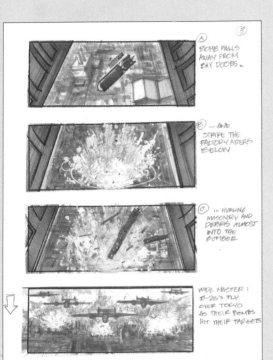

Ⓐ BOMB FALLS AWAY FROM BAY DOORS

Ⓑ ...AND STRIKE THE FACTORY AREAS BELOW.

Ⓒ ...IN HURLING MASONRY AND DEBRIS ALMOST INTO THE BOMBER

WIDE MASTER: B-25's FLY OVER TOKYO AS THEIR BOMBS HIT THEIR TARGETS

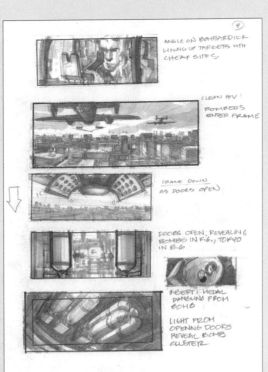

④ ANGLE ON BOMBARDIER LINING UP TARGETS WITH CHEAP SITES.

CLEAN POV: BOMBERS ENTER FRAME

CRANE DOWN AS DOORS OPEN

DOORS OPEN, REVEALING BOMBS IN F.G., TOKYO IN B.G.

INSERT: MEDAL DANGLING FROM BOMB

LIGHT FROM OPENING DOORS REVEAL BOMB CLUSTER

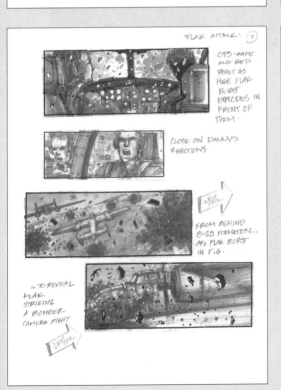

FLAK ATTACK: ⑦

CTS: RAFE AND RED REACT AS HUGE FLAK BURST EXPLODES IN FRONT OF THEM.

CLOSE ON DANNY'S REACTIONS

FROM BEHIND B-25 FORMATION... AS FLAK BURST IN F.G.

...TO REVEAL FLAK STRIKING A BOMBER CAMERA RIGHT.

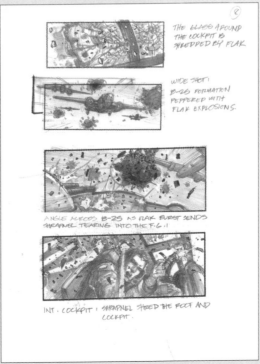

⑧ THE GLASS AROUND THE COCKPIT IS SHREDDED BY FLAK

WIDE SHOT: B-25 FORMATION PEPPERED WITH FLAK EXPLOSIONS.

ANGLE ACROSS B-25 AS FLAK BURST SENDS SHRAPNEL TEARING INTO THE F.G.!

INT. COCKPIT: SHRAPNEL SHRED THE ROOF AND COCKPIT.

In creating the attack sequence, we had two key words: "speed" and "violence." We wanted to make the horror of the attack contemporary. Very early on in the process, Michael and I bashed out things we thought would look kinetic on screen and blast right by you. We played with plastic planes to imagine the point of view of the pilot. We wanted to see ourselves through the eyes of the people on the ground and in the water and put the camera in places you would not want to be during the attack.

Michael always brought us back to the human element and rejected whatever pulled you out of the moment. For example, I had this idea about crashing a plane into a hanger that Michael turned down. He didn't want anything that was James Bond or *Star Wars*. I think Michael invested more heart in this movie than anything he's ever done. There was no limit to what he was willing to show. Technology was no limit. ILM (Industrial Light & Magic, the post production company) never said no to anything we proposed.

—ROBERT CONSING
STORYBOARD ILLUSTRATOR/
VISUAL CONSULTANT

Before I had a script, I started creating storyboards—this was about two weeks after we started developing the idea for the movie. At this stage, I worked mostly on the battle scenes. Storyboards help me write the action scenes and are a way to sell the movie.

—MICHAEL BAY

The bombing of Tokyo is done all in miniature. We construct these 1/8 buildings and then set up on a lot about 75 feet wide and 150 long. For the background plates of Tokyo, we shot a steel mill near Gary, Indiana, which was built in 1902 and looks just like the aerials of Tokyo in the early 1940s.

—MICHAEL LYNCH, SUPERVISING MODEL MAKER
INDUSTRIAL LIGHT & MAGIC

after their plane ditched in the sea, and Corporal Leland Faktor died bailing out with his parachute. Lieutenant Ted Lawson was badly hurt after his plane ditched near the Chinese coast, but he and his men made it to shore and to a hospital. Fortunately, the only medical doctor in the raid, Dr. White, was nearby and could get to Lawson and the others. He had to amputate Lawson's leg to save his life, and gave two pints of his own blood in the process.

Eight men were captured by the Japanese, interrogated and tortured. Public outcry over the attack was ignited by newspaper articles that described the raid as "inhuman, insatiable, indiscriminate

bombing" under headlines such as ENEMY DEVILS STRAFE SCHOOLYARD. In the midst of this fury, the eight crewmen were tried and sentenced to death. Three were executed by firing squad—Lieutenant William Farrow, Lieutenant Dean Hallmark and Sergeant Harold Spatz. In an act of imperial "leniency," the sentences of the remaining five were changed to harsh imprisonment. Lieutenant Robert Meder died of malnutrition in prison, and the others were released after the war. After landing in a field near Vladivostok in the Soviet Union, Captain York and his crew were held by the government. Even though the Soviets were our allies, the men were held prisoner for 14 months until they escaped to Persia (now Iran).

News of the Tokyo raid spread

throughout the country in triumphant headlines such as TOKYO BOMBED: DOOLITTLE DO'OD IT! and in Alaska, NOME TOWN BOY MAKES GOOD! The Japanese gave up pursuit of the carrier task force after two days and were totally bewildered as to where the planes had come from. The operation was still shrouded in secrecy, and President Roosevelt added to the mystery by suggesting that the attack had been launched from "Shangri-La."

The Army flew Doolittle to Washington where a surprise meeting awaited him. Outside President Roosevelt's office, Doolittle was overjoyed to be reunited with his wife, Joe. They were escorted into the Oval Office, where the president shook his hand "long and hard." General Marshall read the citation for the Medal of Honor,

and President Roosevelt pinned the medal on Doolittle's shirt. After telling Roosevelt about the raid and saying thank you to everyone, they were ushered out. Doolittle was thrilled to receive the award, but on his way out he made it clear to General Arnold that the honor wasn't his alone. "I couldn't resist telling him that while I was grateful, I would spend the rest of my life trying to earn it. I felt then and always will that I accepted the award on behalf of all the boys who were with me on the raid."

RIGHT: Bill Skinner added notes to this diagram indicating where to best wreck the plane for the Doolittle Raiders crash landing in China. ABOVE: The crew preps the plane wreckage right before filming in Newhall, California. FAR LEFT: Michael Bay directs Josh Hartnett in a scene filmed on an aircraft carrier.

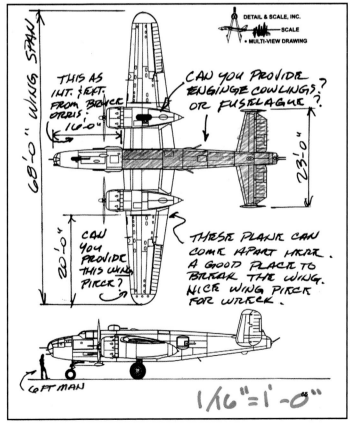

ABOVE: *The Corpus Christi chapter of Pearl Harbor survivors with Josh Hartnett.*
BELOW RIGHT: *The Hawaii chapter poses with producer Jerry Bruckheimer.*

Richard Fisk was the bugler on watch on the *West Virginia* on Sunday morning, December 7, 1941.

I sounded first call for colors at about five minutes to eight. And that's as far as I got. I went over to the port side of the ship and saw a lot of airplanes coming in. We took the first three torpedoes at five minutes to eight and were blown across the ship, which was about 108 feet wide. The captain came up just shortly after eight o'clock. Then there was a tremendous explosion on the number-two gun turret on the *Tennessee* [moored alongside the *West Virginia*] and a big piece of shrapnel almost cut Captain Bennion in half. We took care of him as much as we could.

Finally someone ordered to abandon ship. We fought our way forward through the smoke and the fire. Then we dove off the bow and swam around the *Tennessee* to Ford Island, which was only about forty yards away. I remember there was a lot of fire, and I swam very fast. It seemed like just a short time after that that I was crawling onto land.

There were men in the water who had been blown off the *Arizona*. We got the wounded out first, and then we went back. There were a lot of bodies floating in the water, so we brought them ashore and laid them alongside the beach by the officer's quarters.

Robert Diggins, Seaman First Class, had planned to drive around the island with some of his navy buddies that Sunday. He was parked at the dock across from the *Arizona* when the attack began.

The first time I knew something was wrong was when I got

Early on in prep, I started to interview survivors. While talking to the first man I met, I noticed that his eyes welled up. He kept saying, "I can't forget the screams of the men in the water." I realized this man was telling me a story he rarely shares with anyone. I learned that the survivors of Pearl Harbor don't tell these graphic stories very often—the emotions are just too overwhelming. One of the things I kept hearing from them was that they wanted kids to learn about Pearl Harbor, and they wanted people to remember.

—MICHAEL BAY

blown off the jeep. They dropped a bomb right there on the docks, and it just blew me right out of the jeep. That is when I first started to lose my hearing. I watched the planes come in and bomb the *Arizona*. She got hit several times. I was still there on the dock when the one bomb went down and hit the magazine, and she exploded. It was like a big mushroom, and the concussion from that blew me over again. That was one hell of a concussion.

I got a hold of another sailor and the two of us started pulling men out of the water and off the dock. Anyone who was wounded we started putting on the jeep. The men were burnt, oily, bloody; some of them were in real bad shape. We took them to the hospital directly behind us. We went back and forth all day; there were a lot of wounded. It was a horrible smell and sound, and what really got you was the dead bodies and half bodies. That was the first time I had ever seen a dead person.

THE SURVIVORS

Seaman First Class Louis Nockold was aboard the USS *Honolulu* when the attack began.

When I heard "Battle stations on the double!" on the announcing system, I started running to my gun station, mumbling all the way, "of all the times to have a drill, on Sunday morning." Just as I cleared the hatch and went topside, I looked back over the stern of the ship. There was a plane coming straight at me. It had these big red spots on the wings. I realized, my God this is no drill! Then that plane exploded. The USS *Bagley*, a destroyer that was right around the end of the pier from us, had its guns ready for gunnery exercises on Monday morning. And it had one hell of a good gunner as far as I'm concerned. He opened fire almost immediately. That plane just disappeared—he hit the bomb or the torpedo, whatever the plane was carrying, and it exploded.

When the first lull in the battle came, there was quite a bit of smoke around. We could see that the battleship *Arizona* was on fire. The most startling thing was seeing this great big red thing sticking up out of the water. We couldn't figure out what in the world it was. Then we found out it was the bottom of the USS *Oklahoma* after she had capsized.

I have one living grandfather and one who passed away. They fought against each other in World War II. One is American and the other Hungarian. My Hungarian grandmother, who is Jewish, was in hiding during the war and I asked her if she remembered Pearl Harbor. She said, "Yes, I know where I was that day. I was underground in Budapest. When we heard about the attack over the radio, I'll tell you this, I never thought I'd live to have a granddaughter in a Hollywood movie about that day. That never even occurred to us so far away. It's so strange that you are in this film. I just hope you do it justice. It's a time nobody really wants to remember unless it's remembered right." I actually have a cousin who died on one of the ships that day. I didn't realize it until I went to the memorial and saw his name. My mom told me I was related to him on my grandfather's side.

—CATHERINE KELLNER, ACTRESS

ABOVE: Michael Bay poses with survivors of the Doolittle raid, (left to right) Chase J. Nielsen, Lt. Col. USAF (Ret.), Michael Bay, Henry Potter, Col. USAF (Ret.), Richard E. Cole, Lt. Col. USAF (Ret.). BELOW RIGHT: Jerry Bruckheimer and Michael Bay with the San Diego chapter of Pearl Harbor survivors on the Baja set.

The survivors were very, very protective of Doolittle. They clearly felt he was a great leader and they loved the man. They would not stand for any little derogatory note in the script about Doolittle. Even after his death, Doolittle inspires amazing loyalty among his men.

—JERRY BRUCKHEIMER

Howard Snell quit high school in his senior year to join the Navy.

We had a young history teacher who thought Hitler was the greatest thing since sliced bread. So one day I politely told him, "Well, you like him so well, why don't you go to Germany and take care of him?" He says, "'You're out." So I joined the Navy.

I was attached to the carrier USS *Enterprise* at Pearl Harbor and was going to cooks and bakers school at the base in December 1941. That morning as I was walking out, I Looked across the bay and saw that the *Oklahoma* was hit. She started rolling over. They told us to get some guns, so I went down to the armory and they gave me a Springfield rifle. I just had on my skivvy shirt at the time, and I tell you, I looked like a real bandito. The planes flew right over Ford Island and started their torpedo run. They kept coming, and I was shooting. I didn't hit anything. But I tried. I guess that's the name of the game, try.

It was just mind-boggling to me. I couldn't believe what was happening. It wasn't fear; it was anger more than anything. Of course—nobody could touch us. We're the greatest navy in the world. Nobody's going to come close to us. So, when all of a sudden they do, anger builds up. I was angry. I just couldn't believe it.

Lewis L.A. Gesse, a 19-year-old Navy student aboard the USS *West Virginia*, narrowly missed being taken for dead after his ship was hit.

When they sounded general quarters I went to my battle station on the main deck in the Fourth Division, which is the port side of the ship. I looked out the porthole and saw torpedoes coming in and hitting below decks. All the pipes were bursting with water, oil, gas, steam; everything under the sun. The deck was getting messed up, and I had to get up against the bulkhead to keep from falling down. That's the last thing I remember until I woke up four days later in the hospital ship, *Solace*.

I found out later that the entire deck I had been standing on blew apart. I don't know if it was a bomb or a torpedo from below, but the deck where I last stood was completely gone. They told me that they piled up the dead bodies on the starboard side of the ship. From there they took them off and buried them. A chief who was picking up bodies from this pile called out, "This guy's still alive. He moved an eyelash. He's still alive." So they sent me to the hospital ship, *Solace*, and a dentist sewed me up. There weren't any doctors available, so a dentist stitched up my head wounds.

About the time I woke up, the rescued sailors from the *Oklahoma* were coming in to the *Solace*. They thought they'd been down below deck for a few hours, but they'd been there for about four days. They had no concept of time or hunger or anything because they were completely in shock.

THE SURVIVORS

Seventeen-year-old Manuel Garcia was assigned to the USS *Argon* in 1941, training to be a Navy radioman. When he heard the radio announcement for all military personnel to return to their base, he ran to his ship, which was moored at 1010 dock at Pearl Harbor.

When I got there the planes were again attacking, the second wave was coming in. I was ordered to help haul a canvas down on the dock because they were bringing survivors up from the battleships. They would just take them from the boats and throw them on the dock. Literally! Then the officer on the dock yelled to me, "Get in that whale boat and go pick up survivors." I said, "But I've never been on a whale boat before!" He just ordered me again, "Get now!"

"Yes, sir!" I said, and jumped in the boat with a kid who worked in the *Argon's* central office. I sat at the rudder and he figured out how to be the engineer. We headed for the *California* and started picking up guys out of the water. The first time I came back I kind of rammed into the dock, but in about forty-five minutes I could make that eighteen-foot whale boat do anything I wanted it to do!

The one time I almost lost it was when we were out there pulling guys aboard. I was on the stern, at the rudder, and this guy had one hand on the gunwale and he couldn't get up by himself. So I reached down to grab his left hand and under his arm to lift him up onto the boat. My hand came up—and it was just holding cooked meat.

The whole part of his arm just came off in my hand. I was paralyzed for a little bit. I looked at the guy and he looked at me. Never a sound. Then I reached down and grabbed him by the back of his shorts, lifted him up and threw him in.

Both my grandfathers fought in the Second World War, so meeting the survivors and getting to hear their stories was very inspirational for me. The survivors are the people I really want to satisfy with this movie. It would make me feel really good if they are able to see the movie and say that in some way we showed the world what they really went through.

—*BEN AFFLECK*

CREATING THE FILM

RE-CREATING THE MOMENT

IN THE WATER

The aftermath of the attack at Pearl Harbor was shot at Rosarita Beach, the Fox facility that was built for the filming of *Titanic*. Here, construction crews built the mast and hulls of the *Arizona*, the *West Virginia* and the *Oklahoma*. The ships were narrowed slightly and the ship parts were constructed at 85 percent scale. "Everything we did was huge," says Greg Callas, the construction coordinator. "There was rarely a piece of steel that one or two men could pick up by themselves."

The mast of the *Arizona* presented one of the greatest challenges as it sank into the water at an angle. "We had this piece of steel that weighed about 100,000 pounds that we had to build upright and then lower down at an angle. That was a major endeavor," Callas says. Archival photographs of the tilting mast are among the most haunting and well-known images from Pearl Harbor, so it was important that it be reconstructed with precision and authenticity.

Attention to detail was paramount in all the construction at Rosarita Beach. The mast for the *West Virginia* was architecturally different from that of the *Arizona*, a younger ship.

The crew also had to build the bow section of the *Oklahoma* on a gimbal that was capable of simulating the ship rolling over. "The *Oklahoma* rolling over is one of the biggest set elements because we needed to see it physically lift up and slam down on top of the water," says Nigel Phelps, the production designer. "We started off with illustrations and then made a foam core model with a simple pivoting mechanism. From there, the project just got more and more refined.

"John Frazier made a computerized version and then Michael could decide exactly what movements he wanted to achieve. Originally, we had it just rotating, but when Michael decided he wanted it to come out of the water and slap down, that made it very complicated for John. As none of

The facility at Rosarita offers a clear horizon with an unobstructed view out to sea. The only other facility with this kind of view, that I know, is in Malta. Rosarita is a three-hour drive from L.A. and an hour by plane, so we could go down there and make sure things were up and running.

—BARRY WALDMAN, EXECUTIVE PRODUCER

135

Early conceptual drawings by Guy Hendrix Dyas. ABOVE: *Rollover of the USS* Oklahoma. RIGHT: *Interior of the* Oklahoma *from the crew's perspective.*

this had been done before, it involved working closely with John and Greg. Unfortunately, you really can't appreciate the engineering aspects of this as it is all hidden under water."

At 150 percent scale, the *Oklahoma* took eight weeks to build. The hull rose 25 degrees and rolled over with 150 men hanging on and falling off.

None of the materials needed were available in Mexico, so everything had to be shipped from Los Angeles, which presented enormous problems not only with transportation but also with customs. Still, from all accounts, it was well worth the effort. "The highlight of the Rosarita set was the rollover and seeing it turn for the first time. All these stunt men jumping off as it went over. It was staggering," claims K. C. Hodenfield, associate producer and first assistant director, who documented the event with his own camera. "Thirty seconds later, the ship is righted, the men climb back and it's ready to turn again. It was phenomenal," he adds.

We had about two weeks to do the work in Mexico. *Titanic* was there for over a year. Our work in the tank was huge. When the stunt people were bailing off the ships, you had to make sure that the choreography was structured in such a way that the first row out would stagger in a certain pattern. The second row would either go center, far or front. There were three positions. The third row had to pick a spot where somebody else already went down in the water. There was a ring in the water they had to jump into to avoid landing on the previous jumper. Unlike other shows, we didn't have a lot of time to rig a bunch of wires. It was just bodies raining down from the air, falling one after another, after another, after another. We would shoot these sequences three to six times. Every once in a while Michael [Bay] would say, give me five guys on fire. If *Armageddon* had a thousand elements to it, *Pearl Harbor* had a million.

—KENNY BATES, ASSOCIATE PRODUCER/STUNT COORDINATOR

FAR LEFT: *Foreground setup for the* Arizona *and the* Oklahoma, *positioned so that the camera can get long shots.* ABOVE: *Photo shot at Rosarita Beach showing the gimbal that made the ship roll over and the cameras coming into the shot on an aerial cable.* LEFT *and* RIGHT: *Constructing the two enormous structures that will then be placed in the water.*

Our shots were huge and the chances for mistakes were immense. We did one six-ship explosion that was rigged for over a month-and-a-half, and it had an EPA report three inches thick. There were over 450 separate bombs that had to be detonated within seven seconds of each other, and they had to go off one second after the planes flew by. It went off flawlessly. I was operating one of the cameras and I got a little shaky because

I could not believe the massive size of the explosions. They were the biggest explosions I've ever seen, possibly the biggest ever created for a film.

—MICHAEL BAY

ABOVE: *Michael Bay in Baja in a photo that shows the scale of the set.* LEFT: *The stunt crew.* RIGHT: *Bruce Hendricks, Executive Producer and John Frazier, Special Effects Supervisor.* FAR RIGHT: *Jerry Bruckheimer photograph of (from left) Les Tomita, Key Grip, Harry Humphries, Tech Advisor, and Kenny Bates, Associate Producer/Stunt Coordinator.*

This sequence of Ben's plane going down in England was shot in a 15-foot-deep tank in Rosarita, Mexico. Ben is supposed to be dazed and confused and he gets caught in his parachute. This was a surreal, dreamlike sequence. To shoot the scene we had 2 divers bring Ben down into the tank. He's in full wardrobe and is breathing through a long hose until we set up the shot and get the lighting done. I have the camera on him at all times and, to my left, is an underwater electrician who has two fluorescent lights on Ben's face. We start filming when Ben lets go of the regulator and we shoot until he signals for air. Each shot is about 20-30 seconds and we keep doing it, probably longer than we should, until we get the shot.

—PETE ROMANO, UNDERWATER
DIRECTOR OF PHOTOGRAPHY

UNDER WATER

ABOVE: *Pete Romano shooting under water as drowning sailors float past the sunken* Oklahoma. *Photo by Chip Matheson.* BELOW: *Concept drawing by Warren Manser of the underwater attack showing sailors clinging to the coral reefs to avoid strafing from the Zeros. This incident is re-created from accounts of Pearl Harbor survivors.*

My number-one concern throughout the entire movie was the safety factor. I wanted to make sure that no one got hurt and, and, fortunately, it was a very safe movie. We had a remarkable stunt crew and a remarkable marine crew that kept everybody in the water safe. My other concern was that I just didn't want us to sink a ship. I thought that might be bad publicity —to sink a ship in Pearl Harbor.

—Bruce Hendricks,
Executive Producer

ABOVE: *Ben Affleck being filmed under water.*
BELOW RIGHT: *Polaroids shot by costume designer Michael Kaplan of the uniform Affleck wears in the underwater scenes.*
BELOW: *Pete Romano, underwater director of photography.*

143

They just don't make pictures this big anymore. Michael designed the most incredible images for the battle scenes. I shot in the water from the POV of the struggling, drowning victims. I was dressed as a sailor and my camera was camouflaged with canvas. I was between two huge destroyers with these Zeros bearing down on us only fifteen feet off the water. Guys on fire were jumping off the ships and debris was everywhere. It was Michael's playhouse. I worked on *The Rock* and *Armageddon,* but this was the most-fun movie experience I've ever had.

—PETE ROMANO, UNDERWATER
DIRECTOR OF PHOTOGRAPHY

INSET: *Guy Hendrix Dyas's concept art
"Dead Angels."*

In the fourth day of photography, we were planning to explode 300 bombs on six ships. I was driving down the highway and there, in front of me, was the reserved fleet. And I'm thinking, somebody is going to be driving down this road on their way to work and they're going to see six ships engulfed in a massive fireball and we're going to have a 30-car pile up. We're going to have to close down two Interstates. Two minutes before we set off the explosions the Highway Patrol of Hawaii stopped traffic.

—K. C. HODENFIELD, ASSOCIATE PRODUCER/FIRST ASSISTANT DIRECTOR

I started taking photographs when I was six or seven years old. Later, in high school, I won some awards but I kind of got away from it to establish my career. I still love photography and, because of the visual treats on this film, it was a natural thing to pull out a camera and start taking pictures again. Michael's got such a great eye that whatever he sets up is easy to photograph; he made me look really good with the photographs I took.

—JERRY BRUCKHEIMER

ABOVE and LEFT: Getting the strafe marks in the water required special rigging to get the effect as shown on left and in above photo by Jerry Bruckheimer. RIGHT: Jerry Bruckheimer shooting on location in Baja.

The exact right airplanes for this movie are not available at any price. The Zero that we are using, for example, is a later model Zero, but it's the only flying Zero in the whole world. The other two Zeros that we are using have been refitted with American engines just so they could be flown. When we're flying the Zeros, we're in what might be called the "Disney Formation," which is a formation we devised to look good on camera. It's not necessarily a real formation that you'd fly. The reality is that we have other factors—such as camera angles—to consider.

—STEVE HINTON, CHIEF PILOT

Alan Purwin, the aerial coordinator, and I arranged for sixteen vintage airplanes from various sources to be delivered to North Island San Diego, with the Navy's cooperation, but then we had to ship them to Hawaii. The planes were wrapped in plastic—shrink-wrap it's called—to protect them from the elements. We loaded them onto an oceangoing barge, lashed them down and waved good-bye. They were on a twelve- to fourteen-day trip all alone.

It was quite a gut grinder for a week or two because updates on their progress were scarce. But then we got to Hawaii and the Navy took us out on a P3 Orion and flew us over the barge. They were still two hundred miles off the coast but we could look down from the sky and see our little white airplanes on the deck of this barge. My heart just started pounding.

We descended to get a closer look and, even though the planes were out at sea for eleven days, they looked just like when we left them. That was a big highlight of my career just to be out there in the middle of the Pacific—blue as far as you can see—and look down and see these planes!

—STEVE HINTON, CHIEF PILOT

RIGHT: *Fifteen Zeros were constructed for the movie.* ABOVE: *The Zeros were shrink-wrapped in plastic and loaded onto an aircraft carrier for shipment to Hawaii.*

BELOW: *The aerial crew plots the flight course of the planes. From left, mechanic Matt Nightingale, pilots John Hinton and Tom Camp, ground support crew member John Curtis Paul and chief pilot Steve Hinton.*

This movie is by far the most technically advanced airplane movie ever made. There are filmmakers who'll say we could've done all the planes with computer graphics (CG). But there are things that you get from using real planes. First of all, they give a rush to the actors on the ground. But also, the camera picks up nuances. We were using older planes—they slide, they do little weird things. Once you have these real planes in the shot and then incorporate the CG planes, you're able to establish a realistic, true-to-life impression of how these planes fly. I strongly believe that an audience subconsciously knows a real plane from a fake plane. Still, I feel that CG planes have never been so successfully utilized in a film as they are in *Pearl Harbor*.

—MICHAEL BAY

LEFT: Photo by Jerry Bruckheimer.
INSET: Alan Purwin, aerial coordinator, and Jerry Bruckheimer. ABOVE and RIGHT: Michael Bay directing on set.

It was just one enormous shot after another enormous shot on a big backdrop. All hell is breaking loose on the runway. Bombs are blowing up. Planes are coming at you at 200 miles per hour. All the time, six cameras are rolling and 150 guys are running around creating mayhem. We're shooting six days a week, all day, and it never stopped. It just took your breath away.

—K. C. HODENFIELD, ASSOCIATE PRODUCER/FIRST ASSISTANT DIRECTOR

We had the best pilots in the world working on this movie. Michael had them flying over explosions, he had them flying ten feet off the ground with high tension wires and power lines everywhere. You name it, these pilots did it, and in planes that were sixty years old.

—JERRY BRUCKHEIMER

I'm not a pilot, only an admirer and very respectful of pilots, but when you climb into one of those old planes, you realize it's just a big bucket. These are dated planes. You can see out the windows but you can't see over the front of this plane. You can look out the side but you can't see what's down below you. Until you go up inside one of those planes, you can't understand what the pilots deserve for their aerial stunts.

—KENNY BATES, ASSOCIATE PRODUCER/STUNT COORDINATOR

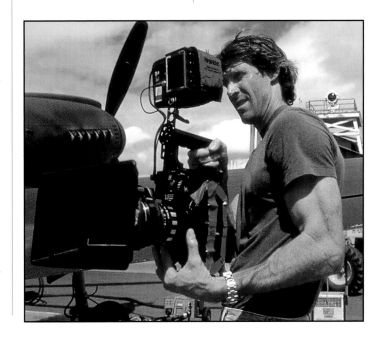

151

Michael wanted to simulate a plane moving realistically. We didn't want something that would just shake the camera or something on a platform that would vibrate. No, we wanted the plane to do as many maneuvers as possible. So we went to the guys who built the gimbal for the rollover and they created a similar gimbal that would elevate a plane. I think it was about 38 feet in the air and could spin 360 degrees. It gave the plane the same fluid movements as in flight, and between the camera, the smoke and the wind we could make it really look like the guy is flying.

—BARRY WALDMAN,
EXECUTIVE PRODUCER

At Pearl Harbor in 1941, our fleet of planes was on the tarmac when the Japanese attacked. In our story, the boys are trying to get back to their planes, so to simulate that, we needed a fleet of P-40s, which are no longer around. There are maybe three or four still in existence. The construction department took a mold of one of the planes and duplicated it so that we had 15 mock-up aircraft. But Michael wanted to take it a bit further than just having the planes sit there on the tarmac. So we had these real propellers made and hooked them up to hydraulic motors so they would spin. We could actually move them out on the tarmac without anyone in them and it looked like they were getting ready to take off.

—JOHN FRAZIER
SPECIAL EFFECTS SUPERVISOR

At the end of this long crane was a turntable that allowed the cockpit to pitch, yawn and rotate. It was like an amusement park ride for the actors. Everybody was clamoring to get in the cockpit and do three-sixties.

—BRUCE HENDRICKS,
EXECUTIVE PRODUCER

Working on this big Hollywood movie was like a baptism by fire. It doesn't get much bigger than this. It felt like there were five movies going on at once. In Hawaii, sometimes there were four different units shooting at the same time. I can't imagine what it was like to direct this movie, it must be terrifying.

—KATE BECKINSALE

The most impressive thing to me was the people who flew the fighter planes. They pretty much worked together. They got into unison and would do their passes and then they did big loops and came back around. In the middle of that, out of nowhere, pops this helicopter with all the cameras and it suddenly dips down. I thought, oh my gosh, those are the bravest men on the set. It was really intense to watch.

—CUBA GOODING, JR.

This is as good as it gets for an actor. You're actually in Pearl Harbor and there are real Zeros coming over you and you are in a 1937 Buick. It was awesome.

—JOSH HARTNETT

ON FIRE

We blew up seventeen ships in the harbor. Michael [Bay] said that we had to blow up real ships. Every other movie that's ever been made would use models and it would look bad. But Michael really stepped up to the plate and said either we do it the right way or we don't do it.

It took months and months for the lawyers to pull this off. We had to go through the Department of Defense, the Navy and all the environmental groups in Hawaii. We signed off on every environmental group whether it was plants, turtles, birds or the smoke we put into the air. We were environmentally correct from the start and we stayed that way through the whole movie.

To blow up the ships, we strategically placed high-explosive charges where they would do no harm to the ship. We did everything we could to protect these ships and, in the end, all we did was a little smoke damage.

Apocalypse Now was two years in the making. *Tora Tora Tora* was a year in the making. We did what they did in five weeks on this picture.

There's an old cliché that if it was easy they would've hired a relative.

— JOHN FRAZIER
SPECIAL EFFECTS SUPERVISOR

ABOVE: Stuntman on fire during attack scene. BELOW: Warren Manser illustration of the ships on fire in the harbor. RIGHT: Barry Waldman, K. C. Hodenfield, John Schwartzman and Michael Bay on location. BELOW RIGHT: Bruckheimer on location in Mexico.

We occupied a lot of Ford Island which is an historical landmark. We had to be very careful with the environment. We were prepared to stop filming if a sea turtle came passing through the frame.

—BRUCE HENDRICKS,
EXECUTIVE PRODUCER

Everything we did in Mexico and Hawaii, we did big. Our 30 days in Hawaii would have been 90 days in any other circumstances. In Hawaii, we had 50 gallons of fuel with primer cord around them. Each explosion was 100 feet around in a circle, and we set up 20 of those explosions that would progressively come towards the lens.

We put our stunt people in between these explosions. Some of the biggest explosions I've ever seen. We had jeeps with guys in them swerving away from exploding bombs. There were a lot of shots where, if you were looking the wrong direction or you made a wrong turn, the result would have been very ugly, if not fatal.

We were constantly on the go. It was like a little factory of people going out and doing explosions over and over. It was Michael Bay pace. It was beyond challenging, it was our own battle to get through the day. I've worked with Michael for ten years but I've never had to work quicker or be more creative in my entire life.

We did so much in Hawaii that it is almost like a dream now.

—KENNY BATES, ASSOCIATE
PRODUCER/STUNT COORDINATOR

Ben [Affleck] knows that working with me is sometimes madness, confusion, and utter chaos, but I use those things to my advantage, especially in the battle sequences. I remember the first battle shot we did with Josh—I pulled Ben aside and said, "We're gonna blow up that DC-3, and it's gonna be huge and loud." For the scene, they had to drive the car and then jump out, so I told Ben, "You make sure you put Josh's head down so that we know he's safe, and then we're gonna rip the hell out of this place with the strafing and the explosion." As soon as the explosion goes off, Ben picks up Josh and starts running. And Josh looks truly scared.

We had lots of new actors who did not have much movie experience, and they were asking, "What exactly am I supposed to do?" I said, "You know what, you're in a war, you don't know exactly what you're supposed to do. I'm not gonna tell you everything." Do you think the sailors at Pearl Harbor had someone to tell them what to do during the surprise attack? My actors would look at me like I was being unfair. But then we'd start firing guns and blowing up bombs around them, and they reacted perfectly—because just as at Pearl—it was the first time they'd ever been around explosions.

—MICHAEL BAY

The stunt people come from all walks of life. They're members of the Screen Actors Guild. A lot of these guys are professional athletes, ex-athletes, rodeo cowboys, high divers, or gymnasts. They're professionals who are very proud of what they do.

I take my job very seriously but we are like a bunch of gypsies. We've known each other for twenty years and we come together to make these huge films and blow things up.

—KENNY BATES, ASSOCIATE PRODUCER/STUNT COORDINATOR

We used mostly military for extras, which started in Hawaii with the military requesting we use their personnel on the base. And from day one, it was great to work with guys whose lives are about taking orders. You tell them where to stand and they're happy to do it.

We had Navy Seals in the water and these guys didn't even want to wear wet suits. "Yes sir, can I stand here in the water for another 60 minutes while the planes are flying over my head?" All you have to do is feed them and they want to come back because they're having the most fun.

In Mexico we used military guys from San Diego and more Navy Seals. They looked great in uniform and they had the right haircuts. They lent authenticity to the movie.

—K. C. HODENFIELD,
ASSOCIATE PRODUCER/FIRST
ASSISTANT DIRECTOR

BELOW: Michael Bay shooting on location.

When the pilots are up there everybody has to be in sync. If the planes aren't in the picture when the explosives go off, then there's no sense in doing it. So you wait until all the planes are in formation.

My crew and I go back to before *Apocalypse Now*. We are all governed by the state of California and we have a license that is issued by the state after a pretty extensive test on explosives. One of the state's requirements is that you must be in line-of-sight of your explosion. You must be able to see what is going on. When you have multiple explosions, you have multiple pyrotechnicians.

This is the biggest picture we've done to date. At times, we had up to 75 men on our crew.

There was so much that could go wrong but we managed it without a hitch. We are very proud of our safety record on this movie.

— JOHN FRAZIER,
SPECIAL EFFECTS SUPERVISOR

157

ON FIRE

This is the biggest movie I've ever attempted to make and the hardest movie I've ever had to mount for a number of reasons including the cost and getting commitments from the talent that was involved. But when you look at the movie, the vision is enormous. It's bigger than anything I've ever seen onscreen. It's a throwback to the forties, to David Lean; it's romantic, it's exciting. It's a film that you haven't seen for sixty years. I think it's Michael's tour de force, an amazing piece of filmmaking.

—JERRY BRUCKHEIMER

More than 8,000 military uniforms were manufactured for the filming of *Pearl Harbor*. According to costume designer Michael Kaplan, these included:

MANUFACTURED

1250	Undress whites
250	Dress whites
600	Chambray shirts and pants (Navy)
200	Marine khaki uniforms
200	Navy khaki shirts and pants
300	Army khaki shirts and pants
20	Period flight suits
125	Wool shirts
80	Leather flight jackets
60	Flight helmets (leather and cloth)
75	Choker white uniforms (Navy officers)
25	Chiefs (White uniforms)
120	Pairs of white shoes (leather soles)
200	Pairs of brown shoes (leather soles)
80	White nurses' uniforms
35	White pinafores
25	Navy nurses' sweaters
300	Pairs of white seamed hosiery
40	Doctors' scrubs
40	Doctors' smocks
100	RAF uniforms, flights suits, jackets, boots
	Officers' hats
	Sets of pin insignia and ranks
	Hawaiian shirts
	Period baseball caps

RENTED

4,000 classic military uniforms
Period nurses' dress blues
Flight goggles
Oxygen masks
Parachutes
Harnesses
Flotation vests
Flight equipment
Period boxer shorts and T-shirts
Japanese helmets, goggles, flight suits
Japanese high command uniforms for their Navy and Army
Chinese Amy uniforms
Japanese Underwear

I did a lot of research for the Hawaiian shirt that Ben wears during the bombing scene. Hawaiian shirts have very specific designs. They started becoming novelty items in the 1930s and the patterns then were very simple. In the 1950s designs were more elaborate and more colorful. During the Vietnam war, there was a strong Asian influence.

In *From Here to Eternity*, Montgomery Clift wears a Hawaiian shirt that's actually a 1950s design, even though the movie takes place, like ours, in the early 40s. We were more accurate than that. I had a 1930s fabric reprinted and then we made about a dozen shirts because Ben goes through a long sequence in that costume as Pearl Harbor is attacked.

—MICHAEL KAPLAN, COSTUME DESIGNER

LEFT: *Michael Kaplan, the costume designer, on the set at Baja.* ABOVE: *Ben Affleck wearing the Hawaiian shirt Kaplan discusses on this page.* BELOW: *Affleck in the military costume designed by Kaplan and shown in the designer's original drawing.* FAR RIGHT: *Michael Bay directs Jon Voight who is wearing the suit designed by Kaplan.*

IN WARDROBE

The innate challenge of *Pearl Harbor* was the magnitude of the production. Over the course of the film, we had a multitude of costumers—seamstresses, tailors, agers (people who distress costumes to show the effects of warfare), launderers, shoppers, dressers, design assistants, researchers and military experts in Hawaii, Los Angeles, Texas, Mexico and England. We had to buy, rent and manufacture over 8,000 military uniforms. We bought and rented hundreds of pieces of vintage clothing from the late 1930s and early 1940s for the background extras in the film.

Military uniforms, helmets and insignia were constantly being updated and replaced during the early years of the war. In 1941 (the year of the bombing), the military was still wearing what we would consider World War I helmets (they were changed in 1942). It wasn't until the U.S. was engaged in the war that the uniform we recognize as that of World War II was created. The uniforms in any given scene were slightly mismatched to varied shades of khaki because the fabrics would have come from assorted lots from different parts of the country. We used dyes and washing methods to achieve this kind of color variation. This was very expensive and time consuming but it added richness and reality to the film.

The hardest part of the shoot was the beginning in Hawaii. We had to make sure the costumes matched (continuity wise) in all the scenes. Some of the aftermath scenes were shot before the battle scenes and so we needed to guess at what the damages were. After a shot, many of the actors were covered in soot, grease and movie blood from head to toe. For the next day's work the costumes had to be cleaned (for sanitary reasons) but still look the same. We couldn't send the clothes to a dry cleaner and tell them to remove the smell but not the stains. It was a nightmare. We worked around the clock. My brilliant crew often looked exhausted and filthy, like they were casualties from another war.

—MICHAEL KAPLAN,
COSTUME DESIGNER

For the women's clothing, Michael [Bay] wanted us to push the idea of America's innocence so we went with a late 1930s look, as opposed to the more sophisticated 1940s—for example, a softer, puffed sleeve instead of the more rigid, heavily padded shoulder of the forties. We manufactured the nurses' white uniforms. There was no dress uniform for women until 1942, so we were free to design their street and evening wear when they were not in the hospital on duty.

Another huge challenge was finding period shoes. Women today are a lot bigger than they were in the 1940s, especially their feet. Some of our nurses wore a size 10 or 11—those shoe sizes just didn't exist at that time. We were calling costume houses in New York, London and Italy to send us their larger sizes.

—MICHAEL KAPLAN,
COSTUME DESIGNER

Michael Kaplan's original sketches of the costumes worn by Kate Beckinsale and James King, along with photos of these outfits. BELOW: Seamstresses at work on Beckinsale's gown for her love scene with Hartnett (above).

We had a dedication at the *Arizona* with some of the people from the Navy. The head of the Pacific Fleet gave a little speech and Michael and I gave a speech and then they played "Taps." I think everybody lost it when they played "Taps." Eleven hundred men are entombed underwater. A lot of their shipmates want to be buried with their friends so they get encased in the *Arizona* also. Apparently it happened a few weeks before we got there—a few more men were put with their shipmates. The sacrifices that our armed services made to protect our freedom brings tears to your eyes.

—JERRY BRUCKHEIMER

For some reason, even though it was immense, it was not that hard of a shoot. It was grueling in certain ways, but we were finishing our days early. We were shooting about twelve-hour days, and there should've been huge problems, but there weren't. I think, funny enough, it was because we were blessed by a Hawaiian priest at the beginning of the shoot. It's a law in Hawaii. So we had this priest for the first day. I think the thirty-five minutes he spoke during our shoot day cost us fifty thousand dollars. He put wreaths around us with beautiful flowers. I thought, "Okay, this is going to be five minutes." He spent thirty-five minutes blessing this movie. He was saying how important this movie is to Hawaii, to Pearl Harbor, and to the world. Well, thank God he blessed this movie, because we were working on the water, and we all know what happened with *Waterworld*.

—MICHAEL BAY

ABOVE FROM LEFT: Governor Benjamin E. Cayetano, Admiral Thomas B. Fargo (U.S. Navy Commander in Chief, U.S. Pacific Fleet), Jerry Bruckheimer, Kate Beckinsale, Cuba Gooding, Jr., Josh Hartnett, Michael Bay, Ralph Lindenmeyer (Member Pearl Harbor Survivor Association, San Diego Chapter), and Ben Affleck in the pre-production ceremony aboard the Arizona. *RIGHT: Gaffer Andy Ryan. PAGE AT RIGHT, CLOCKWISE FROM TOP: Three images of Michael Bay on set; John Schwartzman, A.S.C., Director of Photography.*

Before we started filming, we did a memorial remembrance at the actual site on Pearl Harbor. A few of the survivors were there and it was really an emotional thing. Seeing all the names of the men who died there—thousands of them in less than an hour—that plays in your mind.

—CUBA GOODING, JR.

We attended a ceremony at the *Arizona* and, standing over that ship, you can see that it's still leaking oil. It made the whole event feel very present and gave me such a strong sense of the weight of the incident. It left me feeling very awed and reverential about being in that place.

—BEN AFFLECK

We tried to keep the cameras at ground level. If you were running, the camera was head-to-shoulder height. We designed the explosions so that the cameras could run among the stunt men. Once the attack started, the camera was always moving to create a frenetic feeling. Sometimes the stunt men were literally bodyguards for the camera guy in case something was coming at the camera.

—JOHN SCHWARTZMAN, A.S.C.
DIRECTOR OF PHOTOGRAPHY

It amazed me that the story of Pearl Harbor really hadn't been done in a movie. The way the country pulled together and how America rose from the ashes is an amazing story. I was really honored to be allowed on hallowed ground to make this movie.

Pearl Harbor contains an immense amount of real visuals that were done in camera but it also has about 190 digital effects shots. My concept was to make the digital shots huge and do less of them. As a director, I feel you need to have a lot of real footage mixed in with a few digital effects to make it more visceral, make it more realistic.

—MICHAEL BAY

There's a running theme in the movie of my character trying to look after Josh Hartnett's character as a younger brother. Josh is from Minnesota and he has this innocent quality about him that works really well in the context of the period.

Josh is even younger than my younger brother, which really boggles my mind. I think this movie was a little traumatic for him in the same way that I remember *Armageddon* being for me.

—BEN AFFLECK

At first Pearl Harbor looked liked any of the other military bases I'd ever visited. Whoever designed military bases had the aesthetic sense of Henry Ford. You know, you can have any car you want as long as it's black. In this case, you can have any base you want as long as it's beige. They all have this kind of institutional, dull, depressing look. They remind you of high school.

It wasn't until I'd spent about a week at Pearl Harbor that it hit me. Someone showed me these strafe marks and bullet hits that had been left from the Zeros during the actual attack. That's when I realized I was standing in the place where this event actually happened and it was a profoundly moving, emotional realization.

—BEN AFFLECK

CLOCKWISE FROM ABOVE: Art Director Jon Billington, Production Designer Nigel Phelps, Supervising Art Director Martin Laing; fire erupts in the tank in Mexico; photo of photographer Andrew Cooper by Jack Kney; Aerial Director/Cameraman David Nowell, photo by Richard Burton; Ben Affleck between takes. LEFT PAGE, CLOCKWISE FROM TOP: Michael Bay and Jerry Bruckheimer, Josh Hartnett, Jerry Bruckheimer and Josh Hartnett.

ABOVE: *Visual Effects Supervisor Eric Brevig did double duty as second unit director on the film.* RIGHT: *Modellers working on the* Oklahoma *miniature built in exact detail at 1/20th scale.* BELOW: *Battleship Row at the height of the attack. CG planes, boats, water, and smoke were* *added to the shot. The* Nevada *can be seen in the foreground and the overturning* Oklahoma *in the distance. The combination of elaborate CG battleships and smoke simulations made this one of the most complicated visual effect shots ever created for any motion picture.*

We built a 30-foot-long model of a battleship with interchangeable parts so that it could turn into any of the ships on battleship Row. We have different masts and such. The color is altered on computer so we don't have to worry about changing the paint job. We used practical models because the detail holds up well in closeups and for the physical interaction of the smoke with the ship. We can also use them very effectively in underwater scenes that are shot on our practical set where smoke helps create the illusion of being submerged in the ocean. Built to a scale of 1/20th, these are waterline models, meaning there's nothing below the water level.

—MICHAEL LYNCH
SUPERVISING MODEL MAKER
INDUSTRIAL LIGHT & MAGIC

POST PRODUCTION

FAR LEFT: Aerial photography of Pearl Harbor as it was shot for the film. LEFT: Industrial Light and Magic (ILM) composite, which added computer-generated period battleships, aircraft and destroyers. ABOVE: The Ford Island location shot for Battleship Row. BELOW: The same scene after ILM inserted computer-generated ships and sailors. BOTTOM: Dorie Miller (Cuba Gooding Jr.) shooting down a Zero during the attack. The effect of the plane blowing up was created using new simulation software written especially for this film.

When I first read the script, I was overwhelmed by the complexity of what was called for on the page. During the shooting, we were all amazed by what was achieved practically. It's hard to fool an audience. It's hard to make something that wasn't there look real and have it taken for granted. In this movie, the production value on screen is greater than any film I've ever seen. The physical and visual effects elevate this movie to something that looks like it would have cost twice as much to produce.

—ERIC BREVIG
VISUAL EFFECTS SUPERVISOR
INDUSTRIAL LIGHT & MAGIC

ABOVE LEFT: Rafe's plane evades a Japanese Zero in a daredevil aerobatic maneuver through a narrow alley. ILM added the planes, tracer fire and hits on the ground, as well as the building on the right. ABOVE: Original photography of Ford Island Hangar for Rafe's evasive maneuver.

Our job was to add an epic scale to the already impressive live action footage. Michael Bay wants to put everything on the screen that he can. He always wants more smoke, more crashes and more planes. We provide elements that would be impossible to film.

For example, to get the detail of a plane breaking up, we developed a new version of our simulation software without getting an animated feel. We also devised new ways of lighting the material properties of ships and planes.

—BEN SNOW, ASSOCIATE VISUAL EFFECTS SUPERVISOR, ILM

ABOVE LEFT: Lead Animators Scott Wirtz and Scott Benza review animation of the computer-generated sailors featured in the Battleship Row attack sequence. ABOVE RIGHT: Visual Effects Art Director Alex Jaeger and Associate Visual Effects Supervisor Ben Snow discuss concept art for the attack on Battleship Row. RIGHT: Live-action photography of the rotating Oklahoma partial set piece built in Baja, Mexico. FAR RIGHT: The Oklahoma begins to capsize, as sailors swim for their lives and Battleship Row burns in the background. Digital sailors, smoking boats and battle aftermath were added by ILM.

TOP: Model Supervisor Michael Lynch, Co-Visual Effects Supervisor Ed Hirsh, and Miniature Pyrotechnics Supervisor Jeff Heron discuss the destruction of a scale-model of Hangar 54. ABOVE RIGHT: A sequence showing a spectacular plane crash on a battleship during the attack. A stuntman runs as explosions are detonated on the battleship. Computer-generated planes, fire, debris, and background battleships complete the shot.

We had nine actual, flyable planes to simulate the 200-plus needed for the sequence. The audience won't be able to distinguish the real planes from the synthetic, but whenever you see more than nine planes in one scene, you're looking at CG images.

—ERIC BREVIG
VISUAL EFFECTS SUPERVISOR
INDUSTRIAL LIGHT & MAGIC

TO THOSE WHO SERVED US WELL . . .

USS ARIZONA MEMORIAL

The Memorial straddles the sunken hull of the battleship USS Arizona *and commemorates the December 7, 1941, Japanese attack on Pearl Harbor. Spanning the mid-portion of the ship but not touching it, this 184-foot-long structure was designed by architect Alfred Preis and was completed and dedicated in 1962.*

The most symbolic image at Pearl Harbor is the sunken *Arizona*. It's like the *Titanic*, but it's forty feet below water and it's got 1177 men entombed inside. When I first approached this movie, I didn't remember ever seeing any underwater footage and it occurred to me that we had to see the ship as it is today.

The Navy liked the idea of us shooting under water, even though no one had ever been allowed to use the ship in a commercial movie. The National Park Service runs the memorial, and they felt this film would honor the monument and its memory, so they took me on an underwater tour.

I had to put on my diving suit right out there, with all the tourists milling around. I'd dove before, but I couldn't help shaking while I was getting ready. Sixty-year-old oil is still leaking from the ship, which is kind of eerie; it makes these oil slicks on the water. Under the water, it's very murky; there's a lot of silt and green algae. I didn't see anything for a long time, and then all of a sudden there's this huge mass that looks like a barnacle. I saw a porthole with the glass intact. Then I saw the teak deck of the ship. It was just like the deck where we'd been shooting the day before, and that's when the reality of the disaster hit me.

Down farther was a gigantic stairway. The doors were gnarled. There were huge holes in the hull where the ship had been bombed—holes that were the size of a semi-truck. At the front of the ship, there are still three immense guns.

Diving down there made me cry; it was beautiful and scary, and it pulled on every emotional string. It was an extraordinary experience.

—MICHAEL BAY

BACKGROUND: The underwater gun turrets from the USS Arizona *after sixty years on the bottom of the sea. ABOVE: Detail of the wall of remembrance at the memorial in Hawaii. Photos by Pete Romano. FOLLOWING PAGE: Guy Hendrix Dyas's concept drawing of the underwater* Arizona *today.*

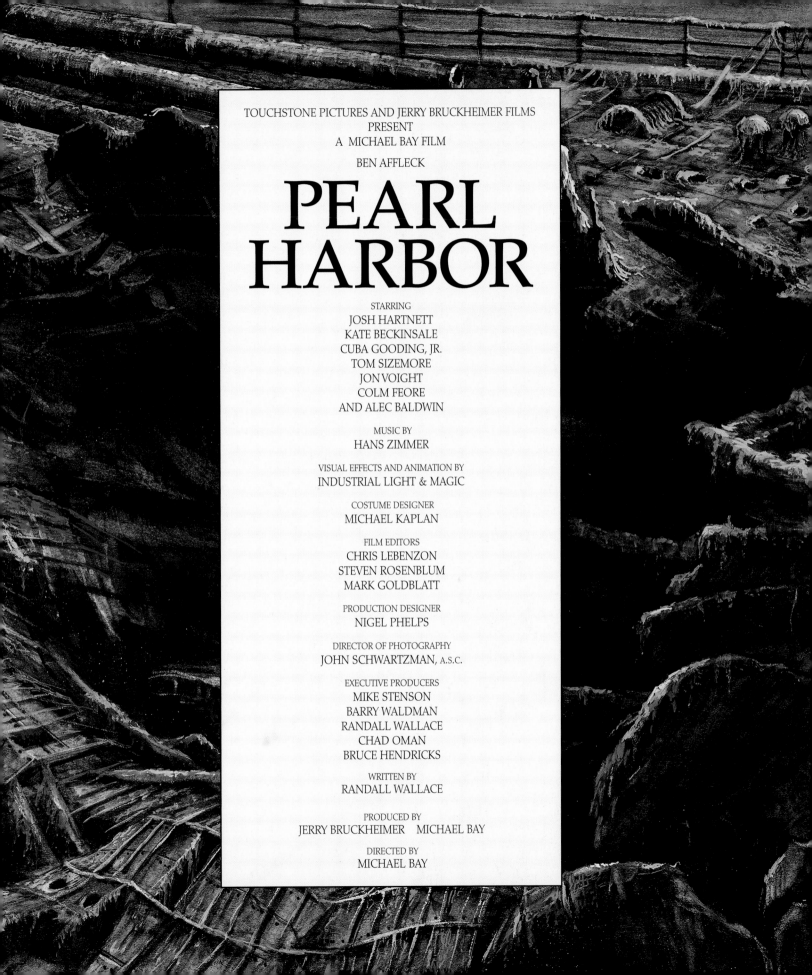

TOUCHSTONE PICTURES AND JERRY BRUCKHEIMER FILMS
PRESENT
A MICHAEL BAY FILM

BEN AFFLECK

PEARL HARBOR

STARRING
JOSH HARTNETT
KATE BECKINSALE
CUBA GOODING, JR.
TOM SIZEMORE
JON VOIGHT
COLM FEORE
AND ALEC BALDWIN

MUSIC BY
HANS ZIMMER

VISUAL EFFECTS AND ANIMATION BY
INDUSTRIAL LIGHT & MAGIC

COSTUME DESIGNER
MICHAEL KAPLAN

FILM EDITORS
CHRIS LEBENZON
STEVEN ROSENBLUM
MARK GOLDBLATT

PRODUCTION DESIGNER
NIGEL PHELPS

DIRECTOR OF PHOTOGRAPHY
JOHN SCHWARTZMAN, A.S.C.

EXECUTIVE PRODUCERS
MIKE STENSON
BARRY WALDMAN
RANDALL WALLACE
CHAD OMAN
BRUCE HENDRICKS

WRITTEN BY
RANDALL WALLACE

PRODUCED BY
JERRY BRUCKHEIMER   MICHAEL BAY

DIRECTED BY
MICHAEL BAY

JERRY BRUCKHEIMER has produced more than thirty films, including *Pearl Harbor, Remember the Titans, Armageddon, The Rock, Crimson Tide, Beverly Hills Cop,* and *Top Gun.* Bruckheimer got his start producing commercials, and not yet thirty, he was at the helm of the cult classic *American Gigolo.* He received the ShoWest Producer of the Year Award in 1998, and in 2000 the Producers' Guild honored him with the David O. Selznick Award for Lifetime Achievement. His films have been honored with fifteen Academy Award® nominations, two Oscars® for Best Song, four Grammys, three Golden Globes, two People's Choice Awards for Best Picture and numerous MTV Awards, including one for Best Picture of the Decade. To date his films have produced more than $12 billion in box office, video, and recording sales.

MICHAEL BAY is the director of three previous movies, *Bad Boys, The Rock,* and *Armageddon.* A graduate of Wesleyan University and Pasadena's Art Center College of Design, Bay got his start in the world of music videos and commercials; he has won every major commercial directing award, including Clios and the Gold and Silver Lions at Cannes. Bay's films have grossed more than $1 billion combined; at thirty-five, he is currently the youngest director ever to reach this milestone. *Pearl Harbor* marks his fourth film.

ACKNOWLEDGMENTS

The publisher would like to thank the following people for their assistance in the preparation of this book: Mark Palansky, Jennifer Klein, Matthew Cohan, and Carolyn McGuinness from Bay Films; KristieAnne Groelinger and Gabriela Gutentag from Jerry Bruckheimer Films; Jill Righty from The Wheelhouse; Michael Mendenhall, Kim Plant, Heidi Trotta, Denise Greenawalt, Holly Clark, Darryl Wright, Renée Stauffer, and Susan Becker from Disney; Chris Measom from Night & Day Design; Vanessa Bendetti; Mark Herzog of Herzog Productions; Randall Wallace; and especially Jerry Bruckheimer and Michael Bay.

Special thanks to Dave Smith of the USS *Utah* Survivor's Association and Jack Green and Robert J. Cressman of the Naval Historical Center.

Jerry Bruckheimer and Michael Bay would like to thank Michael Eisner, Peter Schneider and Dick Cook for their support on the film.

SUGGESTED READING

Air Raid Pearl Harbor: Recollections of a Day of Infamy, edited by Paul Stillwell. Classic collection of first-person accounts.

At Dawn We Slept: The Untold Story of Pearl Harbor by Gordon W. Prange. Based on 37 years of research by the noted historian and naval reservist.

Battleship Arizona: *An Illustrated History* by Paul Stillwell. The full story of the battleship that took the worst hit of the attack.

Day of Infamy by Walter Lord. Minute-by-minute narrative based on hundreds of personal interviews.

December 7, 1941: The Day the Japanese Attacked Pearl Harbor by Gordon W. Prange. Detailed and readable account by historian Prange.

The Eagle Squadrons: Yanks in the RAF, 1940–1942 and *The Eagles' War: The Saga of the Eagle Squadron Pilots, 1940–1945* by Vern Haugland. Two definitive accounts of the Eagle pilots.

G.I. Nightingales: The Army Nurse Corps in World War II by Barbara Brooks Tomblin. First-person stories of activities in the base hospitals during the Pearl Harbor attack.

I Could Never Be So Lucky Again by James Doolittle. The colonel's autobiography includes a vivid retelling of the bombing raid on Japan.

In and Out of Harm's Way: A History of the Navy Nurse Corps by Captain Doris M. Sterne, NC USN (Ret.). The story of Navy nursing, including gripping accounts of nurses on duty during the attack.

No Ordinary Time: Franklin & Eleanor Roosevelt: The Home Front in World War II by Doris Kearns Goodwin. An intimate view of the Roosevelts, from late 1940 through FDR's death in 1945.

The Pacific War 1941–1945 by John Costello. Comprehensive study includes a detailed section about the Pearl Harbor attack.

Pearl Harbor Recalled: New Images of the Day of Infamy. Paintings by Tom Freeman and text by James P. Delgado. A collection of paintings by a renowned artist.

The Way It Was: Pearl Harbor: The Original Photographs by Donald M. Goldstein, Katherine V. Dillon, and J. Michael Wenger. Collection of archival photographs, illuminated by brief biographies and essays.

We're in This War, Too: World War II Letters from American Women in Uniform by Judy Barrett Litoff and David C. Smith. Excerpts of personal letters describe the war experience, including the attack.

SUGGESTED WEBSITES

history.navy.mil [Naval Historical Center] Oral histories, Action Reports from survivors of the Pearl Harbor attack, photographs and more.

navsource.org [NavSource Naval History] Contains a large archival photo collection of the attack on Pearl Harbor, official documents, links and more.

execpc.com/~dschaaf [Pearl Harbor: Remembered] A guide to the USS *Arizona* Memorial in Pearl Harbor, survivor accounts, maps, and links.

pearlharbor.com [*Pearl Harbor*] Visitors to the ambitious *Pearl Harbor* Website can experience Pearl Harbor from several different interactive perspectives, including that of a Japanese spy and an American journalist. Other original features include an immersive 3-D Pearl Harbor experience, a virtual making-of-the-movie tour, and an interactive survivor documentary.

HistoryChannel.com [The History Channel] To learn more about Pearl Harbor and World War II including:

- *This Day in WWII History*: Important or infamous events that happened today or any other day during the year, including Pearl Harbor Day.

- *Dear Home: Letters from WWII*: Get a glimpse of what life was like for soldiers during World War II by reading some of their actual letters.

- *Veteran's Forum*: Join an on-line community where veterans of Pearl Harbor and other conflicts can share their experiences.

SUGGESTED VIDEOS

Pearl Harbor. An in-depth exploration of WWII's most notorious first strike, with archival combat footage, personal accounts and detailed historical analysis. From The History Channel, A&E Home Video, available at retail locations and on the website historychannel.com.

THE HISTORY CHANNEL
WHERE THE PAST COMES ALIVE.